What a wonderful time we have all had helping you Celebrate Your Ruby Wedding Anniversary with lo

Michael, N⌣

WITH A PINCH OF SALT

It is so lovely to be with you to celebrate your Ruby Wedding, & we shall have happy memories of our time together

∞

Lots of love
Reg & Shirley

With a Pinch of Salt

A collection of nautical expressions
and other stories

as interpreted by

Captain Nick Bates

SEAFARER BOOKS

SHERIDAN HOUSE

Published by

Seafarer Books • 102 Redwald Road • Rendlesham • Suffolk IP12 2TE • England
www.seafarerbooks.com

2nd impression 2006

Sheridan House • 145 Palisade Street • Dobbs Ferry NY 10522 • USA
www.sheridanhouse.com

UK ISBN 0 9547062 3 4
US ISBN 1 57409 227 8

A CIP record for this book in the UK is available from the British Library
A CIP record for this book in the USA is available from the Library of Congress

Cartoons: Erik Sansom and Fiona Campbell
Copy-editing: Hugh Brazier
Design and typesetting: Louis Mackay
Text set digitally in Proforma

Printed in China
on behalf of Compass Press Ltd

T he following is a collection of stories, giving my version of the origins of some well-known nautical sayings and expressions. Most are based on fact, although some have the benefit of a little poetic licence. Interspersed throughout are a few stories and little pieces of trivia, all of which I love. These have been gathered over the years, sometimes with the help of passengers and friends, to all of whom I am indebted. It all started on board one ship when I was persuaded by a crew member to share some of these stories during my noontime broadcasts. To my surprise and delight they proved to be very popular. They are basically written in the form I would tell them.

Certain stories are not original to me. Where the author is known, I have been happy to give the credit that is due. If I have not acknowledged the author of a story it is simply because I am unaware of the originator. My apologies if that is the case.

As you will see from page 14, my good friend Patrick O'Shaughnessy has provided me with some of the material. Scattered through this book you will also find some 'thoughts for the day' from the same source. Some of these are serious, but others are perhaps best taken with a Pinch O' Salt.

Nick Bates

Acknowledgements

My thanks go to a few people who have helped
me along the way: Christen Pears, who encouraged me
to start the whole project and helped with the early stages
of editing; Jean Brodie, who helped with so much moral
support and spent many a long evening correcting my
terrible spelling and grammar; Erik Sansom and Fiona
Campbell, who provided such wonderful cartoons;
Patricia Eve, who had faith when I had none;
and Louis Mackay and Hugh Brazier for
spending hours getting it right.

A pinch of salt

FROM THE BEGINNING OF TIME salt was a valuable commodity, not only for the preservation of food but also for enhancing its flavour. This was especially true in warmer countries. Trade routes were established from the coastal regions of the Middle East, where salt water could easily be trapped and left to evaporate in the tropical sunshine, leaving a residue of salt crystals. These crystals were then shipped across deserts and other inhospitable lands to supply the needs of the wealthy further inland.

All this made salt very expensive – but if a meal was to be enhanced it was necessary to add the salt, regardless of the cost.

This was of course was in the days before television, and storytelling was one of the favourite pastimes of the many. A little enhancement or embellishment here and there would often improve the story, just as a little salt would enhance or improve the flavour of food.

This of course would not apply to any of the stories within these pages.

Hammock

A word used to describe the sleeping arrangement of your ordinary sailor on board a sailing ship. A hammock is a piece of canvas or netting strung between two supports, where the occupant could lie in comfort while his bed moved in rhythm with the motion of the ship. It also had the advantage of taking up very little space, could be folded away, and could even used to plug holes made in the ship's side by errant cannon balls.

With all these marine applications, you might suppose that hammocks were originally the product of sailing ships. However, they were first discovered by Columbus when he visited the islands of the Bahamas around 1498. He noticed that the natives used to spend a considerable amount of time resting on woven netting slung between two palm trees. This allowed the occupants to gently sway with the breeze. The local word for these beds became **hamaca** in Spanish, and **hammock** in English.

Brass monkey

In the bygone days of the British Navy, warships carried cannon and, of course, the cannon balls to go with them.

It was always the practice to keep a stockpile close to the cannon. Now, cannon balls, as we know, are round, and if left on deck to their own devices would roll all over the place. In order to prevent this, they were placed inside a brass rectangle, about two inches high, and piled on top of each other to form a pyramid, similar to the way a shopkeeper would display oranges. This retainer was called a **brass monkey**.

Cannon balls were usually made out of cast iron and in very cold weather the brass would contract more rapidly than the iron. If it got

cold enough, the cannon balls would actually fall off the monkey. Hence we arrive at the expression, **It's cold enough to freeze the cannon balls off a brass monkey**.

It was felt unnecessary on naval ships to use the word cannon when referring to cannon balls.

Knowing the ropes

Refers to a person who understands his job or profession. To operate a sailing ship it was necessary to understand the function of, and be able to locate, the hundreds of ropes necessary to control the sails and masts. It took years of experience to become a competent seaman on board a sailing ship, and it was praise indeed when a sailor was described as **knowing the ropes**.

Piping hot

Used to describe food that is very hot and ready to eat. Meal times on board naval ships were announced by the blowing of the bosun's pipe. The pipe was blown as soon as the food was ready and therefore assumed to be hot. Sadly, this was not always the case.

The Beaufort scale

The original Beaufort wind-force scale was devised by Admiral Sir Francis Beaufort in 1805. It was based on the amount of sail a man of war could safely carry with varying wind strengths. The concept was to have a fleet-wide standard in order that the same criteria could be used when writing reports. This would at the very least minimise the tendency for some ships' captains to exaggerate the weather conditions experienced.

Force 0   (calm)
           Man of war has no steerage way

Force 1   (light air)
           Man of war is just beginning to have steerage way

Force 2   (light breeze)
           Man of war all sails set in smooth water, speed 1–2 knots

Force 3   (gentle breeze)
           Man of war all sails set, heels gently, speed 3–4 knots

Force 4 (moderate breeze)
       Man of war all sails set, heels moderately, speed 5–7 knots

Force 5 (fresh breeze)
       Man of war all sails set, heels considerably, speed 7–9 knots

Force 6 (strong breeze)
       Man of war furled royals

Force 7 (near gale)
       Man of war furled topgallants, single-reefed topsails

Force 8 (gale)
       Man of war furled jib, double-reefed topsails

Force 9 (severe gale)
       Man of war furled crojack, treble-reefed topsails, single-reefed courses

Force 10 (storm)
       Man of war close-reefed main topsail and forecourse (storm staysails)

In 1838 the Beaufort scale was adjusted to include descriptions of sea conditions and extended to include winds up to force 12 (hurricane). The changes were:

Force 2 (light breeze)
       $^1/_8$–$^1/_4$ fathom wavelets, glassy crests not breaking

Force 5 (fresh breeze)
       1–1$^1/_2$ fathom waves, some sea spray

Force 8 (fresh gale)
       3–4 fathom waves, crests breaking into spindrift

Force 12 (hurricane)
> Waves over 8 fathoms, air filled with foam and seaspray

In 1912 the scale was changed yet again to give a more precise indication by having each wind force measured in knots:

Force 2 (light breeze)
> Wind speed 4–6 knots

Force 5 (fresh breeze)
> Wind speed 17–21 knots

Force 8 (fresh gale)
> Wind speed 34–40 knots

Force 12 (violent storm)
> Wind speed 64–71 knots

Note: One knot is one nautical mile per hour, equivalent to 1.15 mph. A fathom is equivalent to 6 feet.

Finally (for the time being) in 1955 the scale was increased to include winds of up to force 17, which is 109 to 118 knots – or, as we say today, 56 to 61 metres per second.

This series of changes would tend to indicate what we have suspected all along (despite what the meteorological boffins would have us believe) – the weather is actually getting worse.

Flotsam and jetsam

Two common nautical words whose meanings are often confused with each other.

Flotsam is used to describe the wreckage of a ship found floating in the water and comes from the French word ***flotter***, to float. Jetsam, on the other hand, is used to describe any material that is deliberately thrown overboard, for example, in order to lighten a ship in an emergency. This comes from the French ***jeter***, meaning to throw.

Snotty

A word used to describe junior sailors or midshipmen. It derives from the habit that many had of spending a great deal of their initial time on board crying, or at least sniffling at their misfortune of being taken away from their hitherto safe environment at home.

The uniform jackets they wore were not fitted with pockets and so there was no facility for keeping a handkerchief. The next, and easiest, option was to wipe their noses on the sleeves of their jackets. This habit so infuriated Admiral Nelson that he had three large brass buttons sewn onto the sleeves of their jackets – a practice still in existence with many shipping companies today to indicate the position of cadet or apprentice officer.

Garbled

If something is **garbled**, it is all mixed up and not easily understood.

On occasions it was not unknown for some sea captains, wanting to make a little extra profit, to mix their cargo with useless rubbish or garbage. By doing this, if the buyer was not careful, he could be hoodwinked into paying for more than he bargained for.

Ship's speed

A ship's speed was for centuries measured by tying a length of light rope onto a piece of wood or an old **log**. The wood was then thrown over the stern of the ship and, as the ship moved forward, the rope would run out at the same speed as the ship was moving.

In order to measure the length of rope that went out, especially at night-time, knots were tied at fixed intervals along the rope. It was then simply a matter of using a timing device such as a sand glass and counting the number of knots that slipped through the person's hands.

Note: *A knot is one nautical mile per hour. A nautical mile is 6,080 feet, compared to a land mile of 5,280 feet.*

For the mathematically interested, the knots were spaced at intervals of 47 feet 3 inches, and a 28-second sand glass was the most common instrument used for timing. Before you ask, I have absolutely no idea why these figures were chosen.

Do not disturb

Shortly after a main embarkation on board the *Cunard Countess*, the front desk received a slightly hysterical phone call from a passenger in one of the 4 Deck cabins.

It appeared that the passenger could not find his way out of his cabin. He did however have the sense to realise that, since he had actually managed to find his way into the cabin in the first place, there must indeed be a way out. However, at this particular moment he felt trapped.

As all of the cabins on 4 Deck are pretty much the same, the receptionist asked the passenger to stand with his back to the porthole. He complied. She then asked him to walk forward. He did. When he got to the end of the room she asked if there was a door directly in front of him. He said there was and it led into the bathroom. She then asked if there was another door directly to his left. There was. When asked to open that door, the passenger replied that he could not, as there was a notice on the door handle that said **Do not disturb**.

Bite the bullet

To accept something for what it is, even if not totally pleasant. Prior to the days of anaesthetics, if a sailor was wounded in battle the most common method of helping the injured person overcome his discomfort was to have him bite on a lead bullet. This also prevented him from screaming out too loudly, something that other members of the crew found upsetting. Much of the success of this treatment depended on the sailor having teeth.

Down the hatch

An old sailor's toast or final salute at the end of an evening when the time came to drink up and go home.

Cargo ships are constructed with large openings, or hatches, which are used to gain access to the cargo holds or storage spaces below. If a ship was in particularly rough weather and the hatches were not secure, they could quite easily allow the ingress of large quantities of water. **Down the hatch** became a sailors' way of making an opening for large quantities of liquid for personal consumption.

On occasions, a ship could take in so much water via the hatch openings that it could actually capsize and sink. One presumes the toast would then change to **Bottoms up**.

The Andrew

The slang name given to the Royal Navy, of which the origins are not very clear. Some say it comes from a chap by the name of Andrew Miller, who was reputed to be such a prolific supplier of pressed hands that the Navy was considered by some as the Andrew Miller Club. Others would suggest that a certain Andrew Miller had such a virtual monopoly on provisioning His Majesty's ships that the Navy was said to belong to him.

What is certain is there is no conclusive answer to this puzzle.

Swing a cat

This is an expression that conjures up a wonderful and slightly cruel image of someone standing in a confined space, holding a poor little pussy-cat by the tail and attempting to swing it around without inflicting a mortal injury. Not so, as this is yet another one of those expressions that owes its origins to the small, cramped quarters on board the naval ships of the last few centuries.

Sailors the world over are particularly fond of comparing their accommodation with that of other seafarers, and one of the most often used expressions was, 'My room is so small you couldn't swing a cat in it.' They were, of course, referring to the infamous cat o' nine tails, that harsh and all too frequently used means of punishment on board naval ships.

The heads

The little boys' room on board older sailing ships was referred to as
the heads. This originates from the fact that facilities for such personal
needs did not receive a very high priority from ship owners. As a result,
the most common method of relieving oneself was over the ship's side.

Now, square-rigged sailing ships performed best with the wind
blowing from behind (if you'll excuse the pun), so it was very quickly
established that it was much more palatable for all on board if the
forward part of the ship was used for one's personal business.

As it happened, the forward part of the ship was also the location
of the figurehead, a wooden carving used to ward off evil spirits. So
arose the expression of going to the head of the ship or simply going
to **the heads**.

Toe the line

To follow the party line or do as you are told.

The decks on board ships of the line were made up of a series of
parallel wooden planks, usually about six inches wide, with the gaps
in between filled with a mixture of oakum and tar to make them
waterproof.

Every Sunday on board one of Her or His Majesty's warships, the
entire crew would be assembled, with each group or division of men
assigned to their own area on deck. In order to maintain some form of
order, each group had a deck seam to which they lined up by placing
their toes up to the line. When all crew were assembled the Captain
would read out the 'Articles of War' to remind everyone of their
conditions of employment and the penalty if any of those conditions
were broken or orders disobeyed.

Flogging the clock

A term used today to mean adjusting the clock to allow for the time
difference between various countries. However, it was first used to
describe the actions of young midshipmen whose responsibility it was,
while on watch, to mark the time by turning the sand glass every hour.

Now, watches could be an extremely boring duty, especially at night, and it was not unknown for the young men to tap the glass in order to encourage the sand to flow a little quicker.

If caught, a good clip round the ear was often administered, although the severity of the punishment would depend on whether the person discovering the offence was going on or coming off watch.

Mayday

The international distress call used by ships when indicating they are in serious trouble. The term originates from the French **m'aidez**, meaning 'help me'. Or so all the dictionaries tell us. The French for 'help!' is actually **au secours**, of course.

Elephant steak

The restaurants on board the *Queen Elizabeth 2* (*QE2*) have always prided themselves on the range and quality of food they serve, and when one of the Restaurant Managers noticed a lady obviously having difficulty with the menu, he tactfully approached and enquired if he could help.

The lady was indeed having difficult in making up her mind so, in true *QE2* fashion, the Restaurant Manager suggested that if there was nothing on the menu that appealed perhaps the chef could prepare something else.

'Such as?' asked the lady.

'Well, basically, whatever Madam wishes, this is the *QE2* after all.'

'Anything? '

'Try me, Madam.'

'Well,' says the passenger (with perhaps a twinkle in her eye), 'I have always wanted to try an elephant steak.'

'Of course, Madam. Would that be African or Indian?'

Sand

It is customary when building a new ship to have a number of the crew 'stand by' in the shipyard to oversee the construction and, more importantly, get to know the ship. It is then up to the new crew to take the ship away on its maiden voyage with the knowledge that everything is in full working order. Sadly, this is not always the case. During the first trial voyage it is customary to make up a list of all known and detected defects, and the list is then sent back to the builder so that everything can be rectified under the terms and conditions of the guarantee. Every defect, no matter how insignificant, should appear on this list.

On one such voyage our ship, built in Sweden, sailed on her maiden voyage to Long Beach, California. During the voyage the crew spent much of their time checking, testing and checking again all the various aspects of the ship.

One item quickly noticed was the missing sand from the numerous fire buckets strategically placed all around the ship. With the notification made, a report was duly transmitted back to the shipyard along with all the other detected defects.

On arrival in Long Beach, the ship was greeted with a huge pile of stores, spares and replacement parts, one of which was a large wooden packing case. On opening the case we were amused to see that the builders had kindly air-freighted one ton of sand from Sweden to Long Beach, California in order to close-out the previously mentioned oversight.

The ship was berthed about a five-minute walk from one of the nicest beaches on the west coast of the United States.

Go the whole hog

To go the whole way or to spare no expense.

Food on board ship was limited and often of indeterminate quality and origin. Live animals, therefore, were often carried and used to supplement the diet. Now, if a particular ship was called upon to entertain important local officials, or perhaps if the captain wished to impress his superiors, he would often sacrifice one of these animals by having it roasted and served in all its glory before his guests.

Hogs or wild pigs were relatively common animals found in the forests of England and they adapted well to life on board ship, eating the rough fare that even the crew had no stomach for.

Doughnut (or donut)

The original doughnut consisted of a ring of bread dough, deep-fried and flavoured with molasses or sugar.

It is alleged that the first doughnut was invented by a hungry sea captain who, finding it difficult to eat while steering his ship, redesigned his food so that the doughnut would fit over the spoke of the steering wheel – so that he would always have a ready source of nourishment close to hand.

The bridge

Surprising as it may seem, the term bridge when referring to a ship is relatively new, originating from the days of the early paddle-wheel steamers.

In order for the duty watch to keep an eye on these new means of propulsion it was necessary for the officer on the deck to walk from one side of the ship to the other at regular intervals. This in itself could be a tricky exercise as the decks were often covered with cargo, ropes and all sorts of obstacles.

Some enterprising sailor then came up with the idea of placing a walkway between the two paddle wheels, in effect **bridging** the gap between them. From here it was soon discovered that this platform or bridge formed a very good way of monitoring the progress of the ship and so, with the passage of time, more and more navigational equipment was placed on the bridge in order to allow the officer to monitor what was going on.

Toasts and trivia

Attributed to my friend and mentor Patrick O'Shaughnessy

The following are a number of toasts and trivia I have used during my daily broadcasts on board ship. While they may not all be directly connected to the sea, I have it on good authority that Patrick O'Shaughnessy once had a friend who owned a 10-foot rowing boat in the small Irish fishing village of Ardglass.

Other people may lay claim to some of these toasts but as I have been unable to obtain definitive proof of authorship Patrick has reluctantly accepted the heavy burden of ownership.

May your glass be ever full,
May the roof over your head be strong,
May you be in Heaven half an hour
Before the Devil knows you are gone

May you live as long as you want
And never want as long as you live

May your troubles be less and your blessings be more
And nothing but happiness come in through your door

May you be poor in misfortune, rich in blessings,
Slow to make enemies and quick to make friends

May your right hand always be stretched out in
friendship, and never in want

May the roof above you never fall in
And may your friends below never fall out

May there be a generation of children
from the children of your children

May your home always be too small to hold all
of your friends

May the leprechauns be near you,
To spread luck along your way,
And may the Irish angels
Smile on you this day

May you have warm words on a cold evening,
A full moon on a dark night
And the road downhill all the way to your door

May you have the hindsight to know where you've been,
The foresight to know where you are going,
And the insight to know when you are going too far

May you always have a clean shirt,
A clear conscience,
And a pound in your pocket

May the good Lord take a liking to you,
But not too soon

Tight security

Some time ago while alongside in the port of New York we were paid an unexpected visit by the President of the Company, a rather short man, known to have a rather high opinion of his own importance.

As he approached the security officer on the gangway he was asked for his boarding pass. 'Don't you know who I am?' was the short reply,

'No,' said the security officer.

'I am the President.'

'Go away,' (or words to that effect) said the security officer, 'everyone knows Bill Clinton!'

Touch and go

Meaning it could have gone either way.

If a ship had the misfortune to run aground and was then fortunate enough to lift off again very quickly a person might be heard to exclaim, 'Phew, that was **touch and go**.'

Blighty

A good old colonial word used by ex-pats and travellers abroad to describe England. As India was one of the main countries populated by the migrant British it is natural that a number of words in common usage originate from the Hindu language. Blighty is no exception, as the Hindi word for a white European foreigner is **bilayati**.
Spelling was not a prerequisite for foreign travel so the word soon became written as it sounded.

Above board

Meaning 'legal and proper'. Ships trading around the world would from time to time trade in illegal goods, or on occasions might not wish to declare certain items in order to avoid the dreaded excise duty. Decks on ships were separated by wooden boards, and so legal cargo was placed in full view on top or **above the boards**, while other cargoes would be hidden from sight below the boards.

The launching ceremony

The first record of any launching ceremony is believed to be by the Vikings. They had the distinctly antisocial habit of making a human sacrifice when launching a new ship. It was believed this would appease the gods and so protect their vessel.

Animals were later substituted for humans until around the sixteenth century. After that time the launchers would partake of a glass of wine and then present the goblet or glass to the captain of the ship.

Around the seventeenth century the custom of smashing a bottle of wine against the hull was introduced, usually performed by some lady of social standing, The bigger the boat, the higher the social standing of the lady.

My first boat was launched by the 12-year-old daughter of my next-door neighbour – I was 10. We were both as proud as Punch.

Lock stock and barrel

The original firearms used by armies and navies all over the world came with three basic components: the lock, which was the mechanism used to hold the flint, powder and bullet; the stock, being that part which supported the firearm against the body; and finally the barrel, used to direct the bullet in what was hoped to be generally the right direction.

It was not uncommon for military leaders to order spare parts for their firearms in the form of one or more of the above. However, if the purchaser wanted the entire weapon he would just say something to the effect *complete with lock, stock and barrel*. It was from this expression that the term came to be associated with anyone wishing to order a complete and fully functioning item.

Antigua pilots

The main port of the island of Antigua, located in the northern part of the Windward Islands, is St Johns. It is approached via a long channel marked with buoys.

In the 1980s, and through much of the '90s, the pilot service was provided by two delightful yet completely different gentlemen. The first was local to the island, very black, always smiling, and with a face like a kindly rogue. The second was a white ex-pat from Manchester in England. Slightly unusually, both pilots had the same surname – both were called Green.

As cruise ships approached the pilot station and confirmed their arrival time, the message was often followed by the question, 'Will we be getting Light Green or Dark Green today?'

I should mention that both pilots were equally competent and were well aware of the amusement their names caused the cruise ship industry.

In a pickle

A typical British understatement for someone who has found himself in a bit of serious trouble. When Admiral Lord Nelson died during the

Battle of Trafalgar, the art of refrigeration was not quite so advanced as it is today. In order to preserve what remained of his body, he was placed in a barrel of rum for the journey back to England. The alcohol had the effect of preserving or pickling the body.

Now, if someone at the time was unaware of the fate of Lord Nelson and were to enquire after his health, the reply could well have been, 'He's in a bit of a pickle,' meaning of course that he was very far from well.

It is from this that older sailors would often refer to rum as 'Nelson's Blood'.

Son of a gun

In days gone by, it was often very difficult to find and keep crews to man sailing ships. For this reason, when many of these ships returned to their home ports, the captain was very reluctant to grant shore leave, just in case the crew decided to make a run for it.

However, many of the sailors often had wives and/or sweethearts

ashore so, by way of compensation, the captain would often allow these ladies to come and stay on board the ship.

While certainly not approved of, some of these ladies were perhaps a little freer with their favours than would normally be considered appropriate. Inevitably some became pregnant. This, of course resulted in occasions when the father may not have been known.

Now, the main sleeping quarters on board a navy sailing ship were shared by most of the crew on the **gun deck**, and so where the father of a child was uncertain he became known as the son of a **gun-deck crew**, which was eventually shortened to **son of a gun**.

Whistle blower

While cruising around the eastern coast of the South Atlantic, we had a guest on board who was profoundly deaf but was an accomplished lip-reader. Despite her handicap, she liked to take part in everything and was particularly fond of 'hearing' what was going on behind the scenes. One afternoon during tea time, an officer was strolling through the restaurant and stopped to talk to this lady. He told her about the thick fog the ship had experienced during the previous night. 'Strange!' she said, 'I never heard the whistle blowing!'

It took the officer a few moments to catch on.

Visa

When going to Brazil it is a requirement that guests from a number of countries must have a visa. One passenger, when asked why there was no visa in her passport, immediately produced an American Express card and asked, 'Will this do?'

Shanghaied

The city of Shanghai, located on the eastern coast of China, was one of the main trading ports of the Far East and attracted ships from all over the world. The journey there was long and dangerous, often meaning that a number of the ship's crew did not survive the trip. Others, once they arrived, found life to be somewhat more agreeable ashore than on board their damp, cramped ship with only stale food to eat.

Captains, finding themselves short of crew to work their ships, would resort to any fair or foul means to get replacements. For a small payment, gangs of unscrupulous men would roam the bars and back streets of Shanghai and, if they came across a likely candidate, would either administer a sleep-inducing drug or simply hit them over the head, knocking them unconscious. The next thing the poor chap knew was when he woke up and found himself on the high seas. He had just been **Shanghaied**.

Port and starboard

The word starboard, meaning the right-hand side of a ship, is derived from the early tradition of using a steering board projecting from the right side of the ship near the stern. This was used to control the direction of the ship, a bit like a modern-day rudder. This became known as the steering-board side or later the ***starboard*** side.

Because this steering board protruded from the ship's side, the opposite, or left-hand side, was used for docking the vessel alongside a harbour or jetty, in order not to damage the steering board. As this was the side of a vessel that always went alongside in port, it became known as the 'in port' or simply the ***port*** side.

The ubiquitous brick

Here is a little teaser to work on:

- You are sitting in a boat on a lake and there is a brick lying in the bottom of the boat.

- Now you take the brick out of the boat and drop it into the water.

- It sinks.

What happens to the level of the water in the lake?

Answer later

By and large

An expression meaning *for the most part*, or something that is quite well designed.

To sail **by** the wind means to sail with the wind close to the bow of the ship. To sail **large** means running free with the wind from astern. A ship that was good at sailing in both ways could be described by saying, '**By and large**, she is a fine ship.'

Sun over the yard arm

Your average sailor on a ship of the line was a highly disciplined and well-trained individual, much the same as we are today really. To this end, it was considered inappropriate or bad form to have an alcoholic drink until at least the afternoon.

Afternoon officially starts when the sun has reached its highest point in the sky, generally around noon time.

Yards on board sailing ships (those timber spars used to support the sails) were gener- ally found high up the ship's masts, so when the question was asked: 'Is the sun over the yard arm?' what was implied was, had the sun reached its highest point – because if so it would then be permissible to have a little refreshment.

On certain ships, a great deal of leeway was given in deter- mining if the sun had reached its zenith (or highest point).

Questions passengers have asked

Do the crew sleep on board?

Is that island surrounded by water?

Does the ship generate its own electricity?

How do we know which photos are ours?

Why is the sauna so hot?

Is dinner in the dining room?

What time is the midnight buffet?

Waiting for the lift

On board cruise ships crew members are discouraged from using the elevators. There are two reasons for this. Firstly, to reduce the number of operations the lift has to perform, thus reducing the amount of wear and tear. Secondly, to make lifts more readily available for passengers if and when they require to use them.

On board the *QE2* there could be as many as eight decks for staff to climb during their duties and it was not uncommon for crew members to use the passenger lifts rather than make the long and exhausting climb via the stairs.

On one occasion, two officers were walking along the lower passenger deck approaching the forward stairway and bank of three lifts. As the officers rounded the corner of the alleyway, they spotted two crew members standing with a group of passengers also waiting for the next lift. The crew, on seeing the officers, immediately turned tail and headed off up the stairs at a fine old pace.

Observing this sudden change, one of the officers turned to the nearest passenger and, in a rather loud voice, exclaimed, 'Isn't that just typical of the crew on board the *QE2*? Too lazy to wait for the lift!'

The photograph

Shortly after embarkation a young officer was walking past the picture board displaying images of all the senior officers on board. A lady, also looking at the pictures, remarked to the officer how pleased she was to see that the particular captain in command was one she had had the pleasure of sailing with some eight years ago. She then went on to say how delighted she was to see he still looked exactly the same after all these years. The young officer did not have the heart to point out that it was most probably the same photograph.

Manila

Before the invention of man-made fibres, one of the most common and practical types of rope used on board ship was made from the leaves of the wild banana plant. The advantage of this fibre over hemp was it did not require waterproofing and so was cheaper to maintain and easier to handle. Wild banana plants were plentiful in the Philippine islands and it is the capital Manila that gave its name to this type of rope.

Eight bells

The practice of ringing bells at sea is as old as the bells themselves. On board ship it is important to observe some form of timekeeping to facilitate the smooth running of the ship. As clocks or watches were, at best, expensive and so out of the reach of the ordinary sailor, time was measured by using a sand glass.

It was left to one of the ship's boys or midshipmen to be responsible for turning the glass. The most common form came with a running time of half an hour. As periods of duty were split up into four-hour watches, it quickly became the custom to sound the ship's bell every time the sand glass was turned.

In order to tell the time from the bell, noon, 4 p.m., 8 p.m., midnight, etc. were marked by the ringing of eight bells. Every half hour thereafter was marked by the ringing of one bell, with an additional ring for each subsequent half hour. Therefore 12.30 was marked by one ring, 1 o'clock by two rings, and so on, until eight bells were sounded after the four-hour period. Are you confused yet?

It was also custom that on the change of watch, when eight bells were sounded, and of course provided everything was in order, to shout, '***Eight bells and all is well.***'

Once a year, sixteen bells were rung to mark the end of an old year and the beginning of a new. Usually the oldest person on board was given the task of ringing out the old while the youngest person on board was allowed to ring in the new. This tradition still happens today, especially on board cruise ships.

Aloof

A word often used to describe a person who is very stand-offish or difficult to approach.

On ships sailing close to a lee shore it was considered good seamanship to trim the sails so that the ship sailed as close to the wind as possible. This could considerably reduce the risk of getting too close to the shore and the possible disastrous consequences that would cause. When sailing under these conditions the ship was said to be standing off or sailing aloof. To ***luff*** means to turn a ship towards the wind. ***Loef*** is the Dutch word for windward – apparently.

Chock-a-block

Full, or no more room. It stems from when two ***blocks*** or pulleys rigged together to haul sails come so close together that they cannot be pulled any more.

Shiver me timbers

A lovely traditional nautical expression we all associate with a Long John Silver type telling scary yarns from bygone days.

There is, however, an interesting logic to this expression. **Timbers** was the name applied to the main supports of the deck of a ship. If the ship was in particularly unpleasant weather, it would shudder under the effect of the waves. This caused the timbers to apparently **shiver**, something sailors were not particularly fond of hearing as it had the potential to cause serious leaking – or even worse.

Waister

To call someone a *waster* is to imply that that person is not particularly good at anything or a bit of a waste of time. In fact the word **waist** refers to that part of a ship located on or close to the main deck.

Running a ship required a great deal of physical effort and, as is the case with us all, as we get a little older we are less able to perform some of the more physical tasks we used to. Climbing the ship's rigging required huge amounts of effort and sailors no longer able to perform this duty were given alternative employment, on the decks or in the lower waist of the ship. Here they looked after many of the less demanding yet still important jobs that also required attention. Hence we arrive at the word **waister** (waster in modern English).

As is so often the case, even today, those who were less capable became the butt of the young and abled, not always the smartest of things to do as one of the jobs often assigned to waisters was helping in the galley. A place where subtle revenge was easy to exact.

Bell-bottom trousers

Once the fashion in the 1960s, trousers with flared bottoms were originally designed by sailors living and working on board sailing ships.

Early ships required much swabbing of the decks in order to keep them clean and to keep the hands busy during long periods at sea. It was found to be extremely uncomfortable walking around the ship with wet trouser-bottoms so, around 1817, permission was given for the wearing of the **bell bottoms**, thus making it easier to roll the legs above the knee and keep them dry.

One good turn deserves another

We are all familiar with this expression, and again it stems from the days of sail. To secure equipment on board ship requires tying it down with rope. To make sure the end of the rope was secure, it was often wrapped around *bits*, *bollards* or *belaying pins*. Just to finally make sure, a canny sailor would put an extra **turn** around the bits.

Cuts little ice

We take this to mean something that fails to make much of an impression.

Many sailing ships were built rather like shoe boxes with a very flat, slightly rounded bow. Should these ships find themselves navigating in ice fields, the shape of the bow was not at all conducive to cutting a passage through the ice. Some ships were later designed specifically to make the passage through ice much easier. These ships had a strengthened and much more pointed profile, so allowing the ship to virtually slice a passage through the ice.

Answer to the Ubiquitous Brick

In the first instance, when the brick is inside the boat it is considered to be a floating object, and therefore the amount of water displaced by the effect of the brick in the boat is equal to the weight of the brick. Once the brick is submerged in the water the amount of water displaced is equal to the volume of the brick. As the brick is denser than the water it will displace less water when submerged. So the height of the water will fall.

Splice the main brace

A term used to mean free drinks for all.

The main brace on a sailing ship was a piece of heavy-duty rigging attached to the main yard or sail support. In the event of it parting, making the repair was a pretty onerous task, usually involving most of the ship's company. It was a custom that when the brace had been ***spliced***, or rejoined, the crew were rewarded with a free tot of rum. The expression was later used to signal free drinks for all after any particularly difficult task had been satisfactorily completed, or more especially before and after battle.

The practice of issuing free rum in the Navy was dropped in 1970 – much to the dismay of all hands on board.

The Doldrums or Horse Latitudes

There is an area of the world close to the equator known as the Doldrums. It is generally agreed to be within an area five degrees to the north and south of the equator and is well known for its calm and tranquil sea conditions – all very fine for modern ships but quite disastrous on the sailing ships of yore.

When sailing ships reached this area, they would often become becalmed for days or even weeks at a time, causing a great mood of depression on board the ship. Even worse, it could cause the ship to run dangerously low of fresh water. Many of these ships carried horses belonging to soldiers or passengers leaving Europe for a new life. These horses also required copious quantities of fresh water to survive and, sadly, in order to conserve water for the human cargo, the horses often had to go. Vessels subsequently following these ships would often came across the carcasses of the horses when they reached the **Doldrums**, and so the other name of **Horse Latitudes** came to be used.

P.O.S.H.

Most people are familiar with the word **posh**, which is used to describe someone who is generally quite comfortably off and enjoys the finer things in life. It is said to originate from the days of the British Raj when passenger ships sailed to and from the Indian Subcontinent. Early passenger ships did not have any form of air conditioning and, in the heat of the day, it was always preferable and more comfortable to be in the shady part of the ship.

Ships heading outbound sailed mostly in an southerly and easterly direction, and thus the port side was more shaded, cooler and more comfortable during the hottest part of the day. On the return journey the reverse was true, with the starboard side receiving more shade.

Those who could afford to pick and choose would specifically ask for a cabin on the **Port** side on the way **Out** and the **Starboard** side on the way **Home**.

Extract from the log of Christopher Columbus 1492

'The moon was in its third quarter. Rose in the east shortly before midnight. I estimate we were making 9 knots and had gone some $67\frac{1}{2}$ miles from nightfall. Then at two hours after midnight the *Pinta* fired a cannon, my signal for the sighting of land.'

Believed to be the first recorded acknowledgement of the sighting of America.

Cassini

'It is better to have absolutely no idea where one is and to know it than to believe confidently that one is where one is not.'

A salutary lesson for all navigators.

Clean shoes

One evening, the receptionist on board the *QE2* received a telephone call from a guest in one of the penthouse suites.

It appeared there was some form of problem with the plumbing in the bathroom. It did not take long for the duty plumber to arrive and knock on the suite room door. When the passenger answered the door, the plumber removed his shoes before entering the room – leaving them in the corridor outside – and proceeded into the cabin to fix the problem. After about fifteen minutes all was well and the plumber left. On stepping back into the corridor he bent down to put on his shoes only to find, to his horror, that they had disappeared. Upset and a little confused, he went along to the room service pantry to ask the duty stewardess if she had seen anyone take them.

He found her quietly sitting on a stool attempting to polish what could only be described as a well-worn pair of working shoes. On seeing the mechanic, she held one up and exclaimed how some people were really terribly odd, when they could afford an expensive suite and yet wore such terrible shoes.

Not being one to miss an opportunity, the plumber let her continue until the shoes were once again bright and clean.

Cut and run

To leave quickly. If a ship were at anchor and the captain suddenly found himself in a situation where his vessel was in imminent danger, either from attack by a superior force, or from an impending storm, he could take the decision to cut the anchor adrift and sail off in the most expedient direction.

Their Lordships at the Admiralty were not particularly sympathetic to such a decision in the former case, as it could indicate an unwillingness to meet the enemy in battle.

USS *Constitution*

The USS *Constitution* (*Old Ironsides*) was a combat vessel and carried 48,600 gallons of fresh water for her crew of 475 officers and men. This was sufficient to last six months of sustained operations at sea. However, it should be noted that according to her log, 'On July 27th 1798, the USS *Constitution* sailed from Boston with a full complement of 475 officers and men, 48,600 gallons of fresh water, 7,400 cannon shot, 11,600 pounds of black powder and **79,400 gallons of rum**.'

Her mission: 'To destroy and harass English shipping.' Making Jamaica on 6 October, she took on 826 pounds of flour and **68,300 gallons of rum**. Then she headed for the Azores, arriving there on 12 November, and was provisioned with 550 pounds of beef and **64,300 gallons of Portuguese wine**. (Presumably they didn't have any rum on the islands.) On 18 November she set sail for England. On the way, she defeated five British men-of-war and captured and scuttled twelve English merchantmen, **salvaging only the rum aboard each**.

By 26 January her powder and shot were exhausted. Nevertheless, although unarmed, she made a night raid up the Firth of Clyde in Scotland. Her landing party captured a whisky distillery and transferred **40,000 gallons of single malt Scotch** aboard by dawn. She then headed home, arriving back in Boston on 20 February 1799, with no cannon shot, no food, no powder, no rum, no wine, no whisky and 38,600 gallons of stagnant water.

By my calculations that means the crew drank at least 530 gallons of liquor each during the voyage, or 2.5 gallons per man per day, not counting the quantity removed from the seventeen captured British ships. **What a way to go**!

Minding your P's and Q's

Back in the seventeenth and eighteenth centuries, it was the custom for His Majesty's warships to provide the sailors with regular quantities of ale. This was dispensed in either one-pint or one-quart measures, a quart being the equivalent of two pints.

As is so often the case, after consuming several measures of ale, some of the sailors became a bit overexcited or rowdy.

Whenever that happened the bosun would often attempt to restore order by shouting, 'Mind your pints and quarts!' or simply 'Mind your P's and Q's!'

As an aside, I understand that when the sailors lined up to receive their ration the thirsty ones, rather than ask for a quart, would abbreviate the order and simply ask for a Q. I am not at all sure what the abbreviation was when someone just wanted a pint.

THOUGHT FOR THE DAY

Always look a gift horse in the mouth

PO'S

Slush fund

A term used to describe a pool of money that has a dubious origin.

On board ships, before the days of refrigeration, meat was stored in wooden barrels. When the meat in a barrel was consumed there was a residue of slurry or slush left in the barrel. This was scraped out by the ship's cook and sold on, usually for making candles.

Sometimes the proceeds were used for the benefit of the ship's company but more often for the benefit of the cook.

This also led to another expression, ***scraping the bottom of the barrel***.

Blood money

Pirates were, for the most part, an unsavoury bunch of men and women who would stoop to any means fair or foul to earn a living. Apart from the obvious and well-recorded capturing and plundering of unsuspecting cargo ships, another method of collecting their fortune was to capture wealthy and prominent citizens from many of the local countries they visited.

These captives were then held for ransom and their families were asked to pay handsomely for their safe return. Close relatives have always been known as blood relations, indicating their closeness and bond of true family. When **blood money** was requested it was the relatives of those captured who were approached. A reasonably sure way of getting something back. Well, almost always.

Water-skiing

While cruising in the Caribbean a young officer, well known for his carefulness with money, enjoyed jet-skiing, wind-surfing and water-skiing during any free time he had.

On one occasion, while taking a break in Barbados, he decided to try some water-skiing. On seeing a local boat nearby, he approached the driver and enquired about charges. The driver (apparently not the owner), barely raising his prostrate body from the after seat, replied that it would cost $15 for ten minutes. Thinking this somewhat excessive, the officer apologised for disturbing the driver, declined his offer, and continued to walk further along the beach. It wasn't long before he came across a cardboard sign resting against an old petrol can proclaiming water-skiing at $10 for ten minutes.

However, at that particular moment, there was no boat anywhere to be seen. Forming a cunning plan, he returned to the first boat, where the driver was still comfortably reclined on the boat seat. When he mentioned that the competition was charging $5 less, the driver just told him to go with the other boat. Sadly, the officer then had to confess that the other boat was not exactly there at that particular moment. The driver replied that he, too, charged only $10 when he wasn't there.

Another equator

On a round cruise from Southampton to South America, we crossed the equator on our way to Salvador on the eastern coast of Brazil. King Neptune and his good Lady paid us the customary visit and, assisted by his court officials, initiated all those entering southern latitudes for the first time. After completing our tour of the highlights of South

America we started on our return trip. Two days before our arrival in Dakar on the coast of West Africa, the Hotel Manager received a strong complaint from a passenger who was upset that we were repeating part of the trip by crossing the Equator for the second time in one cruise. She felt we should have returned to England via a different route.

A team of navigators are currently working on this problem.

Hanky panky

A semi-light-hearted expression often used to describe inappropriate behaviour, especially involving someone of the opposite sex.

A century or two ago **hanky panky** was the name given to a mixture of brandy and ginger, at the time rather a potent and popular refreshment, particularly among the higher-ranking seagoing gentry. Having consumed several of these cocktails, perhaps at the house of some foreign dignitary, it was not unheard of for the occasional admiral to make amorous advances towards one of the guests, perhaps even the hostess. A common means of restoring good behaviour was to stop the offender's hanky panky.

Duffle bag

Did you know that the **duffle bag** was the name of the original bag in which sailors used to carry their sea gear around? It originates from the Flemish town of Duffel, where they made the rough woollen fabric for the inexpensive cloth used for sailor's clothing and the over-the-shoulder bag for carrying it in.

Nail your colours to the mast

An expression meaning to make your position quite clear to all concerned. During sea battles, if a ship wished to surrender without further bloodshed the captain would lower her flag or 'colours'. Nailing her colours to the mast indicated that surrender was not an option.

Some nautical terms explained

Anchor	A device for retrieving mud, weeds and discarded cables from the sea bed
Propeller	A device for retrieving ropes, lines and logs from the sea surface
Chart	A large piece of paper used for absorbing coffee spills
Rhumb line	Two or more sailors waiting for their daily tot
Great circle	A really good circle
Starboard	A piece of timber used by navigators in celestial navigation
Port	A rather fine red wine
Stern	A harsh look
Bow	The act of paying homage to someone in a superior position
Bulkhead	Sailor with a large ego
Celestial fix	Something a navigator requires every day
Splice	Type of insect found in rope lockers

Capsize	The internal dimensions of a piece of head gear
Galley	*Roman times*: type of ship propelled by slaves
	Modern times: area of ship operated by slaves (particularly applicable to 'pleasure' craft)
Latitude	The number of degrees off course a captain will allow a new helmsman to steer before interfering
Longitude	The time it takes to relay the message about latitude
Landlubber	Anyone on board a ship who should not be
Heave ho	What a landlubber does when he has eaten too much
Heave to	Two landlubbers who have eaten too much
Displacement tonnage	The act of forgetting where you have left your boat
Gross tonnage	An ugly boat
Net tonnage	A boat with holes
Scupper	A light meal taken while working below decks
Swell	A very nice wave

Weather report

The following is an exact copy of an official weather forecast sent out to ship-ping in the Northern Atlantic:

WEST CENTRAL SECTION
IN NORTH, WEST OR NORTHWEST, 4 OR 5 IN THE SOUTH, 6 OR 7 IN NORTH. IN SOUTH, NORTHWESTERLY 4 IN NORTHEAST, EAST VEERING SOUTHEAST 4 OR 5 IN THE SOUTHWEST. RAIN IN THE WEST MODERATE OR POOR.

Brings to mind John chapter 3 verse 8.

Stateroom

The term stateroom is often used to describe passenger accommodation on board a cruise liner. It derives from the days of the paddle-wheel steamboats that plied their trade up and down the rivers of the United States. The better rooms on these steamers were named after states such as Pennsylvania, New York and New Jersey – hence stateroom.

Coddswallop

A slang term for someone talking a load of rubbish.

Wallop was a popular term for many of the cheaper beer-based products so often favoured by the Admiralty. In about 1875, a certain Hiram Codd invented a form of carbonated soda water. This had the advantage of remaining drinkable for at least a little longer than the normal water supply. For this reason it became very popular with their Lordships as it meant that, instead of supplementing the sailors' drinking water with beer, they could provide the men with the cheaper and less contentious alternative.

Sailors were not quite so excited about this change and showed their disapproval in the name.

The brig

Jails on board ship have traditionally been referred to as **the brig**. This term stems from the days of Lord Nelson who, whenever he captured enemy sailors, would put them on board a small, fast-sailing ship know as a **brigantine** for transport back to wherever. Regular crew members who were found to have committed a serious crime were also put on the brig and sent home to face the mercy of the courts (if they were lucky).

Friday

Traditionally, sailors are a superstitious lot and one of their long-standing superstitions was sailing from port on a Friday. This became such a problem in the seventeenth and eighteenth centuries that the British Admiralty decided to dispel the myth once and for all.

They laid the keel of a new ship on a Friday, launched it on Friday, called it HMS *Friday*, the first captain was called Friday and she sailed on her first voyage on a Friday. Everything worked extremely well – except neither the ship nor the crew were ever heard of again.

Booby trap

A type of hidden trap designed to capture, maim, or even kill unsuspecting adversaries.

The **booby** is common type of seabird not particularly known for its degree of intelligence, probably as a result of too many attempts at trying to catch its sustenance by diving from great heights into the water, thereby repeatedly banging its head on entry. Success rate from this form of hunting has been estimated at about one in eight attempts.

For years, sailors who had the misfortune to find themselves abandoned at sea would catch these birds as a source of food. The simplest method used was to place a scrap of food on a clear area of their survival craft then, using a short piece of string, lay a sort of lasso trap close to where the unsuspecting bird was expected to land. Should the bird place a foot inside the loop the trapper would quickly tug on the string and so secure his prey.

The success rate of this form of hunting was about one in fifty attempts, leaving one to think that the booby bird would have been much better off relying on the temptations of shipwrecked sailors as a means of sustenance.

Scratch my back

'You scratch my back and I'll scratch yours' may seem like an obvious expression, but again we have to thank the British Navy for its origin.

In the days when flogging with the cat o' nine tails was common, shipmates generally administered the punishment to each other. The marks left after each stroke of the cat were known 'affectionately' as **scratches** (a misnomer if ever there was one). When one sailor was due a flogging he would often say to the person appointed, 'If you scratch my back I'll scratch yours.' Now, this could mean one of two things. If the person was heavy-handed he could expect the same treatment if and when his turn for a flogging came, or if the person was kind and light-handed that favour would be returned at a later date.

Bosun

Traditionally the man in charge of the daily workings of the sailors is called the *bosun*.

This name originates from a combination of two words, boat and swain. Sailing ships had a number of smaller boats used to transport officers and crew ashore. One was actually called the *boat* and was basically reserved for the captain. A *swain* is an old English word meaning keeper or 'in charge of'. The boatswain was therefore the man in charge of the captain's boat. Over the years, and for the sake of simplicity, the term has been abbreviated to *bosun*.

On modern ships the position of bosun carries a great deal of responsibility and a vast knowledge of practical seamanship.

The term coxswain is arrived at in a similar fashion but I am not going to go there.

Taken aback

A term used to describe someone who has received surprising or unexpected news, perhaps even leaving them speechless or unable to respond.

Sailing ships relied on wind force and direction if they wished to make any sort of progress across the waters. If either of these natural phenomena were to suddenly change, particularly the latter, it could cause the sails to fill in the opposite direction to the one intended. This could cause unexpected strains on the rigging and was even known to snap a mast or two. At best it would stop the progress of the ship or make it go backwards.

Luck of the draw

Success awaits the sailor who has everything in order. Some people call that *luck*.

Failure is certain for those who have forgotten to take the necessary precautions in time. Others call this *bad luck*.

Attributed in part to Roald Amundsen, 1911

Bully

A term used mostly in school to describe someone who uses his size, strength or power to pray on those less able to defend themselves.

On board sailing ships, the physical effort required to operate the ship was tremendous and it was therefore important that sailors received regular and large amounts of high-protein food – not necessarily good food but food full of protein. One of the most popular vitals of the day was jerky or **bully beef**. Those sailors who ate more than their fair share, and therefore had more energy than their companions, sometimes took advantage of this fact and would prey on their lesser colleagues. They became known as **bully boys**.

Sailors by definition

It is said, 'Sailors work like horses at sea and spend their money like asses ashore.'

Togetherness

Any attempt at getting a group of naval captains to agree on a plan of action is roughly equivalent to that of getting a troop of cavalry horses to pee at the same time.

Quote from Admirable P. O'Shaughnessy, 1781

Letter to the owner

The following letter is attributed to Captain Neil St. C. Norton, whom I would dearly like to meet as I suspect he is a man after my own heart.

Dear Sir,

It is with regret and haste that I write this letter to you; regret that such a small misunderstanding could lead to the following circumstances, and haste in order that you will get this report before you form your own preconceived opinions from reports in the world press, for I am sure that they will tend to over-dramatise the affair.

We had just picked up the pilot and the apprentice had returned from changing the 'G' flag for the 'H', and being his first trip was having difficulty in rolling the 'G' flag up. I therefore proceeded to show him how. Coming to the last part, I told him to 'let go.' The lad, although willing, is not too bright, necessitating my having to repeat the order in a sharper tone.

At this moment the Chief Officer appeared from the chart room, having been plotting the vessel's progress. Thinking that it was the anchors that were being referred to, he repeated the 'Let go' to the Third Officer on the forecastle. The port anchor, having been cleared away but not walked out, was promptly let go. The effect of letting the anchor drop from the pipe while the vessel was proceeding at full harbour speed proved too much for the windlass brake, and the entire length of the port cable was pulled out 'by the roots'. I fear the damage to the chain locker might be extensive. The braking effect of the port anchor naturally caused the vessel to sheer in that direction, towards the swing bridge that spans the tributary to the river up which we were proceeding.

The swing bridge operator showed great presence of mind by opening the bridge for my vessel. Unfortunately he did not think to stop the vehicular traffic. The result being that the bridge partly opened and deposited a Volkswagen, two cyclists and a cattle truck on the foredeck. My ship's company are at present rounding up the contents of the latter, which from the noise I would say are pigs. In his effort to stop the progress of the vessel the Third Officer dropped the starboard anchor, too late to be of practical use as it fell on the swing bridge operator's control cabin.

After the port anchor was let go, the vessel started to sheer and I gave a double ring 'full astern' on the engine room telegraph, and personally rang the engine room to order maximum astern revolutions. I was informed that the temperature was 53 degrees, and asked if there was a film tonight. My reply would not add constructively to this report.

Up to now I have confined my report to the activities at the forward end of my vessel. Down aft they were having their own problems. At the moment the port anchor was let go, the Second Officer was supervising the making fast of the after tug, and was lowering the ship's towing spring into the tug.

The sudden braking effect of the port anchor caused the tug to 'run in under' the stern of my vessel, just at the moment that the propeller was answering my double ring full astern. The prompt action of the Second Officer in securing the inboard end of the towing spring delayed the sinking of the tug by some minutes, thereby allowing the safe abandonment of that vessel.

It is strange, but at the very same moment of letting go the port anchor there was a power cut ashore; the fact that we were passing over a 'Cable Area' at the time suggests that we may have touched something on the river bed. It is perhaps lucky that the high-tension cables brought down by the foremast were not alive, possibly being replaced by the underwater cable, but owing to the shore blackout it is impossible to say where the pylon fell.

It never fails to amaze me, the actions and behaviour of foreigners during moments of minor crisis. The pilot, for instance, is at this moment huddled in the corner of my day cabin, alternatively crooning himself and crying, after having consumed a bottle of gin in a time that is worthy of inclusion in the *Guinness Book of Records*. The tug captain on the other hand reacted violently and had to be forcibly restrained by the Steward, who has him handcuffed in the ship's hospital, where he is telling me to do impossible things with my ship and my person.

I enclose the names and addresses of the drivers and insurance companies of the vehicles on my foredeck, which the Third Officer collected after his somewhat hurried evacuation of the forecastle. These particulars will enable you to claim for the damage that they did to the railings and No. 1 hold.

I am enclosing this preliminary report for I am finding it difficult to concentrate with the sound of police sirens and their flashing lights.

It is sad to think that had the apprentice realised that there is no need to fly pilot flags after dark, none of this would have happened.

Put a sock in it

Without going into technicalities, early gramophones consisted of a revolving disc containing music, a needle to transfer that information and a large horn to amplify any sound. These instruments were very popular on board sailing ships as they did not require electricity to make them work. Now, cabins on board sailing ships were, if they were lucky, divided by flimsy bulkheads; if unlucky by a mere canvas sheet. Sound therefore travelled easily from one section to another. Should someone feel like playing music at a particularly antisocial hour it was not unheard of for a sleepy neighbour to rudely exclaim, '***Put a sock in it!***' – meaning of course to stuff a sock into the horn and so reduce the sound level. Sadly, due to the damp and miserable conditions found on board sailing ships, not many sailors actually owned a pair of socks.

Dutch courage

Meaning bravery assisted by alcohol. First thought to have come into serious use during the Anglo-Dutch wars of the seventeenth and eighteenth centuries. Certain English captains were quick to realise that their crews were inclined to fight (anyone) better after consuming copious quantities of alcohol.

Prior to engaging the Dutch most captains would provide the crew with a hogshead of brandy and so give them the courage to perform their duty.

It seems to have been a fairly effective policy.

The fathom

A nautical unit of measurement equal to six feet, believed to have originated from the old English word **faethm**, meaning to embrace arms.

Your average man was said to have an arm span, from the tip of one middle finger to the tip of his other middle finger, of six feet. The 'embrace arms' is said to come from the amount of arm length a man could extend around the lady of his affection.

St Lucia

The port of Castries on the island of St Lucia is approached via a narrow channel. Mariners are guided into the harbour by a pair of strategically placed leading marks on the hillside behind the town. All very well except that the marks are old, poorly maintained, and very difficult to see – especially when steering into the rising sun.

For years captains had been trying to get the local authorities to make the marks more easily visible – suggesting that all it would take would be a coat of fluorescent paint and a ladder.

After making another nail-biting entrance – still without the help of the leading marks – the captain berated the pilot once again about their condition. Shrugging his shoulders, the pilot just said they did not have the money needed to buy the paint. Without waiting, the captain immediately dispatched me off to the paint store to fetch a tin of our fluorescent paint. On my return, he gave the paint to the pilot on the understanding that the latter would provide the ladder and make sure the marks were painted by our return the following week.

One week later we all stood on the bridge, binoculars poised, searching for the new marks. Nothing. It was not until we entered the port that we noticed a number of houses around the harbour all had newly painted fluorescent-orange front doors!

Taken down a peg or two

Used to describe the process of curtailing someone's ego, and again originating from the days of sail. Admirals had, by tradition, the right to fly their own flag from the highest point on the mast in order to indicate to all just how important they were. The height of the flag was governed by a system of pegs located on the base of the mast and to which the halyard was attached.

Should someone of a more senior rank board the ship then they had the right to fly their flag from the highest point. It therefore became necessary to lower the previous incumbent's flag a peg or two.

Copper-bottom guarantee

The very best form of guarantee.

Wooden ships were/are prone to the ravages of the sea, including running aground, barnacles and nasty sea creatures. If a prudent ship owner wished to protect his investment and in doing so also extend the life of his ship, he had the option of applying copper sheets to the underwater part of the ship's hull. This was extremely expensive and was therefore only considered in the very best and most expensive ships.

Landlubber

The word lubber is believed to date back to the fourteenth century, and is an old English word meaning a clumsy or awkward person. The word **land** was added to **lubber** by sailors around the sixteenth century, and **landlubber** was used to describe someone on board ship who was considered out of place or ill at ease.

The channels

This is an expression used to describe the growing euphoria felt by sailors as they approached the English Channel after a long trip away from home.

In today's Merchant Navy, even though there are crew changes all over the world, the term **the channels** is still used to describe the excitement all crew members feel as it gets close to the time for their well-deserved vacation.

No great shakes

If something is said to be **no great shakes**, it generally means it is not a big deal, or not worth very much.

Food and water were stored in barrels on board ship. When these were empty, and in order to save space, the barrels were broken down, often by shaking. The loose shakes were then stored but were not considered to be worth very much.

Jack Tar

An old name for a British sailor derived from a type of canvas oilskin popular with sailors working on the open wet decks and fashioned to protect them from the elements. To make the canvas waterproof it was covered with a layer of tar and later became known as tarpaulin.

The sandwich

Some ports are not big enough to allow the larger cruise ships to dock alongside and so they must anchor off and ferry passengers back and forth using tenders. This can be quite enjoyable for many guests but is less so for the ship's crew, as it involves almost the entire deck department, engineers, security and hotel staff, all doing extra duties in order to organise the guests, man the boats, keep everything running and provide the additional security ashore and afloat.

THOUGHT FOR THE DAY
A verbal order is not worth the paper it is written on
PO'S

On these occasions it is normal for the security officer to spend much of his day ashore, and this was indeed the case while at anchor off the Croatian city of Dubrovnik. Having already missed his breakfast, and with a lunch break looking out of the question, the security officer called up the bridge and asked if they could ask the chef to prepare something for his lunch. The chef was only too happy to oblige, and it wasn't long before a large tray of sandwiches was making its way ashore. Unable to hand them over to the security officer, who was busy assisting guests, the messenger set the tray down on a nearby table.

After the boat was safely unloaded, the security officer returned to the table eager for his lunch, only to discover that the next group of passengers waiting to embark had found the tray, assumed they were another fine example of Cunard Care, and proceeded to eat the lot.

The final straw for the security officer was when a rather large gentlemen berated him for not arranging to have sufficient sandwiches for all the guests who had to wait those several minutes on the dockside!

Spin a yarn

Meaning a tall tale or someone who tells a good story.

Yarn was the basic ingredient for the making of ropes on board ship. Rope making was considered a relaxing job that did not require a great deal of thought and so, when a group of sailors got together to make up lengths of rope, they would often just sit together and swap old sea stories, some of which, I am sure, got all the better for the telling.

The understatement

Although it smacks of seamanlike efficiency, to say that we heaved up our anchor and sailed out of port is not strictly accurate. It leaves much unsaid.

Attributed to H. W. Tilman (a wonderful and humorous latter-day explorer)

The devil to pay

Basically this is used to mean 'Boy, are you in trouble now.'

On board a ship, the term **to pay** is commonly used to describe the task of sealing planks on the hull, usually with tar. The **devil** was the name given to the seam on or about the waterline. This seam was curved, very difficult to work on, and was therefore considered by all to be an extremely difficult and unpleasant task, one often assigned to someone currently out of favour with the ship's management.

This also ties in with the expression **between the devil and the deep blue sea**.

Ship-shape and Bristol-fashion

In the eighteenth and nineteenth centuries one of the less palatable cargoes transported around the world was that of slaves – a particularly unsavoury period in our history. Due to the appalling and overcrowded conditions on board, ships were often detected by their aroma long before they ever arrived in port.

In Bristol, the local authorities made it a requirement of entry that all such ships should be cleaned and thoroughly disinfected before being allowed to proceed into their harbour.

In addition, when a sailing ship reached its berth the authorities would not grant the crew shore leave until such time as the ship was **squared away**, meaning all spars and yards were to be swung fore and aft to the ship and so avoid the possibility of getting tangled up with other ships berthing close by.

This strict standard was soon emulated by other ports throughout the country and became known as the **Bristol fashion**.

As the crow flies

This expression is used to indicate the shortest distance between two places and originates from the days when navigational equipment was not quite as sophisticated as it is today.

In order to get an indication of the direction of land, the ship would release a crow, which would immediately head off in the direction of the nearest land, thus giving the ship an indication as to its position.

Until quite recently, ships had a lookout platform positioned on the highest mast; this was referred to as the **crow's nest**.

Dog watch

Ships are a 24-hour-a-day operation and it is therefore necessary to maintain a system of watches in order to allow reasonable rest periods for the crews.

To achieve this, the day was split up into six four-hour working periods or watches. A watch keeper would normally stand four hours on duty and then have eight hours off watch. If he was lucky, this might actually be off duty as well. On some ships this would mean that the same watch keepers would stand the same watches, often for long periods at a time, and this could become somewhat tedious. In order to break up the cycle, a system of dividing the afternoon watch into two two-hour periods was introduced. This allowed everyone to rotate duties in the following manner:

12:00 to 16:00	Afternoon watch
16:00 to 18:00	First dog watch
18:00 to 20:00	Second dog watch
20:00 to 24:00	First night watch
00:00 to 04:00	Middle watch
04:00 to 08:00	Morning watch
08:00 to 12:00	Forenoon watch

The origin of the term **dog** is in dispute, but could be linked to **dodging** the daily routine. Another theory relies on the fact that the evening star Sirius, also known as the Dog Star, was generally the first star to appear in the evening sky that could be used for navigational purposes. Between the hours of 16:00 and 20:00 was the time navigators would **watch** for the **dog**.

Over a barrel

Refers to a person who does not have much of a choice.

Drowning, or the potential chance of drowning, was a frequent hazard faced by those who went to sea. Should some careless sailor happen to fall overboard and then be fortunate enough to be rescued, one of the best methods of clearing his lungs was to place the nearly drowned person over a barrel and rock him, not so gently, backward and forward. As time was always at a premium on these occasions, the sailor was not given much choice in this treatment – regardless of how unwell he actually felt.

It should be noted that mouth-to-mouth resuscitation had not been invented at this time, which is probably just as well, as the prospect of administering the kiss of life to a bearded, toothless man suffering from scurvy would not have been all that appealing.

Concorde

Not long after the introduction of the Concorde supersonic airliner, Cunard and British Airways decided to team up to form a partnership, offering passengers a transatlantic crossing one way on the *QE2*, returning via Concorde. This was an extremely attractive offer and, in order to help promote the product, our combined managements decided it would be good publicity if the two 'super liners' were to arrange a radio link-up during a specific crossing. Special radio equipment was installed on board *QE2*; calculations were made; and the approximate time of rendezvous computed.

At the appointed time, just before noon, contact was established. Several of us junior officers gathered around the radio to listen to our captain making history. With the wonders of modern technology, we were able to link up the conversation between the two separate captains who were broadcasting their exchanges over our ship's public address system. It also allowed the passengers to join in this momentous occasion. No doubt the same was happening some 55,000 feet above us.

As the two captains chatted, our captain asked what the Concorde passengers were doing to keep themselves amused during their flight. The reply from Concorde, in a very English public-school accent, went on at some length to describe the meal that was in the process of being served – no doubt in the hope of impressing many of our guests. As he rambled on we knew that protocol dictated he would ask what we were serving our guests for dinner. Knowing our captain didn't have a clue, we hurriedly dispatched a cadet to the Queen's Grill Restaurant in order to fetch a menu.

Unfortunately, the poor lad managed to get lost on the trip and so failed to return in time to be of any assistance. We need not have worried, however, as, without so much as a falter, our captain quietly informed the Concorde pilot how he would love to read out our menu but feared that by the time he finished reading Concorde would be landing in New York. **Way to go, Captain!**

On the fiddle

Meaning to work some sort of scam, primarily for the benefit of the operator.

THOUGHT FOR THE DAY
I am going metric inch by inch
PO'S

On board the sailing ships of yore, entertainment was perhaps not quite as sophisticated as we have on board today's modern cruise liners. Basically anyone who could play a musical instrument was a welcome addition to the crew. The fiddle, being a popular musical instrument of the time, was much favoured by sailors.

Should a sailor be particularly good at knocking out the odd tune he would often be excused some of the more tedious tasks required in the running of a ship, provided of course he played for the crew.

It was not unheard of for a few of the likelier lads to take up the fiddle in order to avoid some of the more unpleasant duties. In other words to be **on the fiddle**.

Rate of pay

A term often used particularly by seafarers when discussing salary or wages. In Nelson's day a seafarer was frequently paid by the size of the ship he served on. As ships were **rated** by the number of guns they carried, the more guns on board the higher the rating and so the more he got paid.

Going flat-out

Meaning to go as fast as you can.

Early marine engines were basic in the extreme and if not carefully handled could over-speed to the point of self-destruction. In order to prevent this and so protect the machinery, a devise called a governor was installed. This was a wonderful adaptation taken from the movement of the pocket watch. It consisted of two, three or even four metal spheres attached to a pivoting arm to form something like a fairground roundabout. The faster the mechanism spun the more towards the horizontal the metal spheres would tilt. Once the arms had reached a preset point this action could be made to activate a device limiting the amount of fuel or steam allowed into the engine, and in this way the speed could be controlled.

If an impatient captain required more speed he would often get the response, 'Sorry, we are **going flat out**.'

Adjustments could be made to allow greater speeds than that recommended – particularly if the chief engineer was going on leave.

Show a leg

This is yet another of those sayings that owes its origins to the days of the sailing ships.

Life was obviously very tough on board the men of war, hence it was often necessary to pressgang men into service. These men, far from being volunteers, would take every opportunity to 'jump ship' whenever they returned to their home port.

In order to prevent this happening, the ships would often anchor some way off the port, making it too far to swim. However, some captains would allow the sailors to bring their wives or sweethearts on board in order for them to be able to spend some quality time together. Sleeping quarters were, of course, at a premium and for the most part confined to hammocks in large rooms where upwards of fifty men would sleep together.

Come morning time, when the petty officers would come to get the men up for work, they knew that many of the hammocks contained both males and females. The normal method of getting a tardy sailor out of bed was simply to tip up the hammock, thereby depositing the occupant onto the deck. However, in order not to upset or embarrass any females, the petty officer would enter the room and shout '**Show a leg!**' If the leg found hanging over the hammock was smooth and silky, then that person was allowed to continue sleeping. Of course should it happen to be hairy and covered in barnacles, then the hammock was tipped over.

So, gentlemen, the moral of the story is, if you want to have a lie-in in the morning, shave your legs.

Hang fire

Meaning to hold on or wait for a short period of time.

On occasions when attempting to fire a cannon it would misfire, or even worse, not fire at all. Should the gunners approach the cannon too quickly there was a possibility that the cannon would suddenly burst into life, with disastrous consequences for anyone who might be standing in close proximity.

In the heat of battle, it was often necessary for cooler heads to keep the firing process under close observation and, should a misfire be suspected, the standard order warning the gunners was to **hang fire**, reminding all concerned to stand clear and wait until it was safe.

Skinned and skint

Dakar, the capital of Senegal, has for centuries been a gateway to Africa. Present-day ships sailing to the east would often use Dakar as a refuelling point and so would call in to fill up before continuing their journey.

While I was serving as a junior apprentice some years ago, we made the customary pit-stop on our way to Australia. Dakar is well known to sailors as a rich place to bargain for local crafts: wood carvings being a particular speciality. On occasion, it was not unheard of to be able to purchase more exotic artefacts.

During our morning break from work while our group of officers were enjoying a cup of tea, we were approached by a local trader. He was offering to procure rare and much sought-after cured lion skins. While this certainly grabbed the attention of a number of us, the trader regretted he could only acquire two such skins in the short time available, each of which would cost the bargain price of $100 US. Much as I was tempted, the sum involved was beyond the dreams of a mere apprentice.

THOUGHT FOR THE DAY
Never drink whiskey with water and never drink water without whiskey

PO'S

In order to guarantee delivery the trader required the money to be paid up-front. Two officers almost jumped out of their overalls in their rush to get to their cabins to collect the necessary funds. Returning almost immediately, they handed over the money to the trader, on the solemn promise that he would return with the goods in plenty of time before the ship sailed.

That was over thirty years ago, and to the best of my knowledge the officers are still waiting.

Turn a blind eye

During the Battle of Copenhagen in 1801 when the British were having a bit of a set-to with the Danish, the then Commander of the British Baltic Fleet, Sir Admiral Hyde Parker, feeling things were not going as well as they should, hoisted the signal for Admiral Nelson to disengage. Nelson, never being one to shy away from a good battle, raised his telescope to his blind eye (lost in a previous battle) and declared 'I really do not see the signal.' He then went on to win a resounding victory. Much to the disgrace of Parker.

The concept of turning a blind eye is still very much in evidence today, especially among some of our more prominent public figures.

Faggot

Faggot was the original name given to a person on board ship who would stand in for an absent colleague during roll call. When the missing person's name was called the faggot would answer 'Aye aye' on his behalf, in exchange for a small sum of money of course.

To miss roll call was an extremely serious offence and could happen for several reasons. Late back from a good run ashore, deliberately not coming back from ashore, or perhaps someone just wanting a little extra time in bed.

Fore

The golfing term **fore** when shouted after striking the ball is meant as an indication to anyone within hearing that the shot just played did not go completely in the direction it was intended, and so serves as warning for others to look out.

During battle, an effective method of maintaining rapid fire with ball and musket was to form several lines of riflemen, or marines if at sea – the idea being that the front line stood ready, then fired their weapons while those behind prepared theirs. When the first line fired, the order was then given '**Beware before**', thus warning the troops in front to kneel or duck out of the firing line of those behind.

As military weapons improved, so did their rate of fire. To say the mouthful 'beware before' started to encroach on the time needed to duck and so the expression was reduced to the simpler *Fore!*

As golf was a favourite pastime of soldiers on leave, the cry was taken up whenever errant balls were struck on the course. This also helps to explain why a stroke with a golf club is called a shot.

The High Sheriff

While cruising the Caribbean we had the dubious pleasure of carrying a gentleman from a well-known city in Scotland. It was his proud boast that he had recently been elected Sheriff of that city.

As the cruise progressed he was gradually making himself more unpopular with guests and crew alike, primarily due to his incessant bragging and complaining. Nothing was quite good enough unless a fuss was made and then only to the highest authorities on board.

On the occasion of the ship's arrival in Barbados, our man booked what was then considered to be one of the finest tours in the Caribbean – a sail on a catamaran, followed by a beach picnic (including refreshment with quantities of local rum) and free horseback riding along the golden sands.

After the picnic, the Sheriff decided it was time to go riding. Summoning a horse and guide, he was gently assisted up and onto the horse. Unfortunately the effort (and who knows the effects of the local rum to those unused to it?) proved a little too much and, instead of remaining on reaching the saddle, he failed to stop and continued over the top, falling rather heavily onto the sand on the other side.

Having lost face and proclaiming he had broken an arm, he immediately blamed the guide, the horse and anyone else close by. Demanding to be taken back to the ship's hospital, he was ushered into a local taxi and promptly returned to the ship for treatment.

On his arrival back on board he was taken to the hospital, where the duty nurse, having been pre-warned, was ready and waiting. She assured him that his arm was not broken. Under normal circumstances this would have been quite sufficient for the majority of guests. Not so the Sheriff, who demanded to see the doctor immediately.

The nurse, who had had enough by this time, picked up the phone, dialled the doctor and exclaimed in a very loud voice, 'Doctor, there is a gentleman down here who says he's a sheriff and he's just fallen off his horse.'

Donkey's breakfast

Something that is a bit of a shambles or all mixed up.

This expression refers to the type of stuffing found in the mattresses used on board cargo ships. These mattresses were stuffed with a mixture of various types of old straw and frayed rope ends, supposedly for comfort – but in practice the contents made the perfect breeding ground for large numbers of unwelcome sleeping companions. One must assume that if the ship carried a donkey the straw and its contents would have made for a well-balanced diet.

Sailors swimming and earrings

It is a well-known fact that very few sailors ever learnt how to swim. There was an obtuse logic to this reasoning that could only be attributed to the devil-may-care attitude of the sailor.

On board a sailing ship, if a crew member had the misfortune to fall overboard, it was highly unlikely that the ship would be able to turn around and rescue the poor soul. Rather than prolong the agony of his time in the sea, watching his ship sail off into the sunset, most sailors opted for the softer option of a quick and relatively painless death by drowning.

The possibility of falling overboard also led to another quaint custom – the wearing of a gold earring. Being the God-fearing Christian gentlemen they were (and of course still are), there was nothing worse than the thought of falling overboard, drowning and being washed ashore on some foreign beach without the prospect of a decent Christian burial.

In case they ever found themselves in this predicament, they wore a gold earring in the hope that whoever found their body would use the gold to pay for the proper funeral arrangements.

An alarming story

From the Night Purser's Report on the QE2:
Two distressed passengers contacted the purser's office to report an alarm sound in their cabin. The passengers stated that the sound was coming from the smoke detector. The night electrician attended the cabin. It was discovered that the sound was coming from their alarm clock, which was packed in their suitcase.

To die for

Many people who cruise seem to derive a certain amount of pleasure in sharing this news with friends and acquaintances.

It is also not unheard of for the occasional guest to book a trip on the *QE2*, or any cruise ship for that matter, knowing it will be their last journey anywhere. In many ways this is not such a bad thing: leaving everything at home in order, sailing off into the sunset, and enjoying your last days simply relaxing. Then when the time approaches just let go.

The only thing that seems a bit sad to me is there is no way you can go home and tell everyone that you just died on your cruise.

Gunpowder plot

A major concern on board naval ships was septicaemia caused by the lack of any form of effective antiseptics for the treatment of wounds and injuries.

Around the mid eighteenth century a rather observant medical practitioner on board one ship happened to notice that during battle gun crews inevitably ended up covered with gunpowder. He further noticed that fewer men operating the guns suffered from septicaemia when compared with other departments around the ship. By way of an experiment, and with the help of the ship's cook, he started to put a small amount of gunpowder into the food served on board. To his delight he discovered that this actually reduced the side effects of many injuries. (There was also a marked improvement noted in the taste of the food.)

Gunpowder, or at least a derivative, is still used in some forms of medical treatment today and is considered a very effective treatment for a number of ailments.

Scuttle butt

A term used to describe gossip, originating from the combination of the words scuttle and butt.

A **butt** was the common name given to a water barrel and **scuttle** meant to cut a hole. A hole or scuttle was cut in the barrel to allow access to the drinking water within.

It was at this barrel that sailors were very fond of congregating to exchange gossip or general news – the eighteenth-century equivalent of the watercooler moment. If a captain wished to know what was happening on board his ship he would just ask a trusted crew member what the **scuttle butt** was, or in other words was there anything he should be aware of.

Personally I have always preferred to hang around the passenger launderette.

Monkey island

This refers to an area on board ship, above the bridge, where the ship's compass was situated. This area was kept clear of obstructions and any unnecessary metal work that could cause interference to the compass. It was also kept free from wandering members of the ship's company.

Now, on board naval ships, young lads, usually between the ages of 10 and 15, used to fetch and carry material, mostly powder, in order to supply the guns during the heat of battle. These young lads were called **monkeys**, or more specifically **powder monkeys**, presumably because of their fondness for getting up to mischief.

It was not unknown for some sailors to try and befriend these young lads, and in order for them to have a relatively safe place where they could gather together, they were allocated the space above the bridge by the compass. Over time this area became known as the **monkey island**.

The term **island** on board a ship refers to a section of isolated deck space.

Flogging a dead horse

A **dead horse** was the term sailors used when they received pay in advance for working on board a ship, usually so that they could leave something behind for their families before setting off to sea.

Flogging a dead horse was when an unscrupulous captain would try to get extra work out of a sailor while he was still working off his debts.

More questions passengers have asked

Will this elevator take me to my cabin?

What time does the 2 o'clock tour start?

Where is the bus for the walking tour?

Will we have time to take the shore excursion?

Are the entertainers paid?

Is the mail brought in by plane?

Who is driving the ship if the captain is at the cocktail party?

Should I put my luggage out before I go to sleep?

Is the trap shooting held outside?

Ship's tonnage

A number of people are under the impression that the gross tonnage of a ship is a measure of the actual weight of the ship. Well this is not the case at all. *Caronia* (a very elegant and popular cruise ship) for example has a gross tonnage of 24,492 tons. This is a measurement originally derived from cargo ships as a means of determining how much cargo the ship could carry and hence its revenue-earning capacity. One ton is equivalent to 100 cubic feet of space that any particular ship can utilise for revenue purposes. Certain areas within the ship are excluded from the calculation, such as crew mess rooms, galleys and some store-rooms, as these are not considered revenue-earning areas. On cruise ships, all passenger cabins, public rooms, shops and dining rooms are included. Areas of open decks are not included.

That is why it can seem a little odd that sometimes smaller ships have a very large gross tonnage while very large ships such as the *QE2* have a relatively low tonnage. New ships tend to be very box-like with lots of cabins reaching out to the extreme sides of the ship. It is the gross tonnage that determines how much ships pay for many of the services at their ports of call.

The word **tonnage** is actually derived from **tunnage** and refers to the number of barrels or tuns a ship could carry. A tun was the most common means of transporting wine.

Jury rig

Meaning something that is temporarily put together to form a make-shift or quick solution to a problem at sea. The word **jury** is an old English word meaning to hastily put together. **Rig** is a term used to describe masts, lines and ropes plus all the other bits and pieces that go together to make up the working parts of a ship. Therefore to **jury rig** something is to make a temporary fix such as would happen in the event of a mast snapping or a rudder falling off.

It is possible there is a connection between the word jury as used in a temporary fix at sea and that used to describe a group of men and women good and true who were hurriedly put together in order to give a fair trial in a court of law.

Grog

A word used to describe alcoholic beverages, usually rum-based.

Back in the days of yore, it was the custom to supply sailors from all nations with copious quantities of rum. Originally produced in the West Indies, it was hoped that by providing sailors with just the right amount it would enhance their performance in battle. It still is a contributory factor in many a skirmish today.

However in 1740, Admiral Vernon (1684–1757) of the Royal Navy decreed that the rum should be watered down, presumably because he felt the neat variety was a little too potent.

The term **grog** comes for the type of cloak that the Admiral wore, known as a Grogram. He was referred to as Old Grog, but not I suspect to his face.

Silence is golden

The bridge on a ship tends to be remarkably quiet when manoeuvring in and out of port, portraying a calmness that can belie the tension that actually exists, especially for the captain as he tends to be the one concentrating most. This outer calmness can be misleading to the uninitiated.

Occasionally guests are invited onto the bridge to share this experience, but it is always on the understanding they do not disturb, or interrupt, any of the duty staff.

During a departure from Rio de Janeiro one such guest failed to grasp the significance of this advice and insisted on disturbing the captain with a barrage of meaningless questions. After putting up with this for several minutes the captain very tactfully asked the lady if she would mind not disturbing him until the ship was clear of the harbour as he was trying to concentrate on the manoeuvring operation.

Apologising profusely the lady went very quiet – for about ten seconds – after which she leant over to the captain again, this time disturbing him completely by asking, 'What manoeuvre are you concentrating on?'

She was the last passenger ever to visit the bridge while he was captain.

Captain Setab's Second Law of Dynamics

In the late seventeenth century Captain Setab of the privateer *Twoeque* discovered that ships had a tendency to roll, especially in rough weather. After a number of years of careful observation he came to the following conclusion:

If a sailor spreads a ship's biscuit (generally with a piece of lard) and it has occasion to fall onto the deck, it will always fall smeared side down. If it fails to do so the seaman has obviously spread the biscuit on the wrong side.

This law does not apply to officers.

SPLORT!

The whole nine yards

Generally taken to mean that someone or something is giving a task everything possible. A typical square-rigged sailing ship had three masts and each mast normally carried three sails. Each sail required a yard to support the upper portion of that sail. That means a typical sailing ship had nine yards. If all sails were set she was said to be going as fast as possible or going **the whole nine yards**.

A loose end

If someone is said to be **at a loose end** it means they are bored or have nothing to do – a recipe for disaster in some circles, especially at sea.

Sailing ships had hundreds of ropes used to control sails and support the masts, each rope had of course two ends, and this made for a large number of ends. If left unattended these ends could become frayed or **loose**, causing them to unravel, look unsightly or possibly foul blocks and rigging.

Any captain **worth his salt**, noticing the crew becoming listless, would call out all hands to inspect and repair any loose ends.

Walking on the moon

One particular captain I sailed with took great pleasure in hosting 'Star Gazer' evenings. These consisted of gathering together a group of budding astronomers and, under cover of the darkness, attempting to explain the origins of the universe.

Under a full moon and with a group of thirty or so passengers, our captain began his lecture. Starting with a description of the phases of the moon, he was just getting into his stride when he heard a voice from the crowd proclaiming, 'Been there!'

Pausing, and not just a just a little annoyed, he turned to the speaker and asked him what he meant.

You can imagine his surprise when Buzz Aldrin, one of the first men to walk on the moon, stepped forward. The lecture took a decidedly different direction from that moment on.

Two fingers

This little piece of trivia is not so much an expression as a gesture, probably one more familiar to the British.

It can best be described as one where a person extends his index and middle finger in the general direction of another person and moves the hand in an up and down motion – now simply known as the two-finger gesture.

I am sure most of us know this is not meant as a particularly complimentary sign, but few probably know that it owes its origin to the battle of Agincourt in 1415, during the reign of Henry V.

It was at this time that the English mustered an army of some 3,000 highly trained longbow-men and set off to fight the French. As all schoolchildren should know, the result was a resounding victory for the English archers, so much so that the French were just a little miffed at being beaten by such an inferior force.

As a result of this, any time the French captured an English archer they would chop off the two fingers that controlled the arrow, thus ensuring he was never able to fire a bow again.

After the battle, all the English archers left bodily intact took great please in displaying their two fingers to the opposition – and hence arose this famous gesture.

Khaki

In the early eighteenth century it was discovered by the British serving in India that if they took some locally made cotton and soaked it for two days in a mixture of mud, coffee and curry powder it came out in a colour that blended in particularly well with the surrounding country-side. This material was then fashioned into military uniforms and has since provided soldiers and sailors with a high degree of camouflage. The only trouble I fear was that the enemy could probably smell the troops long before they came within visual range.

Ladder quiz

If you are on a ship at anchor and you place a ladder over the side so that the bottom rung is just touching the water, if the tide then drops by 27 inches, how many more rungs of the ladder do you have to put out in order for the bottom rung to remain just touching the water? The distance between each rung on the ladder is nine inches.

Answer later

The Alamo

Not much to do with the sea but an interesting story nonetheless

It is well recorded that on 6 March 1836, a contingent of 189 mixed North Americans met and very nearly defeated an army of 2,000 Mexicans at the small area known as The Alamo, located in the southern American state of Texas.

Three of the Americans involved were Jim Bowie, Sam Houston and Davy Crocket, all of whom are credited with originally hailing from Scotland. What is not commonly known is that on the evening before the famous battle the three aforementioned gentlemen spent their time having a bit of a party, during which it is assumed strong drink was taken. This inevitably led to some singing, including one of the most popular and well-known songs of the day, ***Green grow the rushes oh***. As the night wore on, the three men kept singing this song over and over again, much, one must assume, to the annoyance of their opponents. While not understanding the words, the Mexicans were able to recognise the song every time from the title, which started with the words **Green grow**.

It was from this expression that the term **gringo** was formed, and it is now used by Mexicans generally to describe citizens from North America.

Dungarees

The name given to a pair of trousers made from a coarse blend of cotton.

Early traders to India were quick to notice that a locally produced rough cotton fabric made relatively inexpensive replacement sails. Furthermore, once these sails were discarded much of the remaining material could be fashioned into perfectly usable working clothes at little or no cost to the sailors on board ship.

This material, known locally by the Hindi word **dungri**, soon became a popular fabric for the manufacture of working clothes throughout Britain, and the special design of trousers became referred to as **dungarees**.

Warming the bell

To get ahead of things (sometimes mispronounced as 'warning the bell').

Each chamber of an hour glass, used to measure time on board ship, was known as a bell. It was thought – or hoped – by some that if you clasped one or both of the bells in the palms of your hands the heat generated would cause the sand in the glass to flow more quickly, so speeding up the apparent passage of time. This meant that watches on the cold and often wet open decks of a sailing ship would become shorter. Even a few minutes saved was considered a bonus.

I would imagine that if each watch performed the same procedure there must have been some very short days at sea.

Freshen his hawse

Not such a common phrase today but much used by the older generation of square-rigged sailors to describe a person – usually an officer – who after standing watch on a wet and windy deck would look forward to going below for a large tot of rum – *freshen* meaning to wash down and *hawse* in this case being the shortened version of *hawse pipe* or throat in sailor-speak.

First rate

The best. Ships of the Royal Navy were classified by the number of cannon they carried. A ship which carried 100 or more guns was classed as First Rate. Second Rate carried 90–99 cannon, Third Rate 64–89 cannon, all the way down the line to 20 guns, which were Sixth Rate. Ships that did not carry any cannon and were therefore not considered of any great importance were **not rated**.

Magazine

Today this a word used to describe a publication containing all sorts of articles and stories. On ships it is used to describe a room where explosives or weapons are stored. Both words owe their origin to the Arabic word **makhzan**, meaning a place for storing things.

Scot free

Many words in the Scots language are derived from the close connection between the Nordic peoples and Scotland. It was after all those insatiable seafarers the Vikings who did their level best to populate much of the Highlands and Islands of northern Scotland. The Nordic word for **tax** is **skatt**.

In the Middle Ages the government of England imposed a tax, mainly in Scotland, as a means of helping to sustain the war against the Scots. Not surprisingly this tax was quite unpopular, for two very good reasons:

(1) Nobody likes to pay taxes; and

(2) The Scots were not particularly keen on paying for a war against themselves.

Those who did manage to avoid payment were said to get off *skatt-free*.

Martinique taxis

During a Caribbean cruise, as the ship was sailing past the French island of Martinique, the officer on the bridge heard a distress call on the emergency radio frequency. The broadcast was in French – a language he was not particularly comfortable with – but as good fortune would have it the Captain also happened to be on the bridge. A man of infinite resources, the Captain considered himself a moderate French speaker, based on once having spent a two-week holiday in Brittany.

As they listened to the broadcast, it became apparent to the Captain that the distress call was coming from a ship that had broken down, required immediate assistance, and the crew were in a state of imminent starvation.

Summoning the emergency parties out of their beds to prepare the rescue boats, all hands eagerly awaited further orders. Since the Captain was aware that the crew of the stricken ship were, from all accounts, extremely hungry, he also summoned the Hotel Manager to the bridge and ordered him and his team to prepare to feed any rescued seamen – however many there might be.

As the Hotel Manager arrived on the bridge, still half-asleep and not in the best of humour, the distress call was clearly heard over the radio once again. The two senior officers listened intently to the broadcast. When it had finished, the Captain turned to the Hotel Manager and asked if he could determine any clue as to the whereabouts of the distressed vessel.

The Hotel Manager, having lived in southern France for a number of years, was quite conversant with the language. Taking a deep breath, he advised the Captain that the call was from a taxi driver on Martinique. Apparently his cab had broken down, and he wanted his controller to send for a tow truck then call his wife to let her know he would be late home for dinner and would be really hungry.

Getting steamed

A colloquial expression used primarily north of the border to describe someone who is either heavily under the influence of alcohol or someone whose intention is to become so.

In and around the city of Glasgow at the start of the twentieth century, one of the most popular forms of relaxation was to take one of the local steamships for a cruise up and down the River Clyde – or as they would say locally *doon the waater*. In order to encourage the public to participate in this particular form of relaxation, and presumably to enhance the coffers of the steamship owners, copious quantities of relatively cheap alcohol were provided for the duration of the cruise.

On completion of the outing, assuming of course it was completed, many of the participants could be seen making their way ashore with varying degrees of competency – hence the expression ***getting steamed***.

Answer to Ladder quiz

As the ship is floating in the water you do not have to put out any more ladder for the height to remain the same.

Going off at half cock

Meaning to react to something prematurely, often without fully weighing up all the implications. In the seventeenth and eighteenth centuries guns were fired by first pulling back on the firing mechanism – known as **cocking the gun**. The exercise of cocking was in two stages. The first stage was the **half cock**, when the hammer was pulled back halfway, leaving the gun almost ready to fire but still supposedly in a safe mode. The second stage was the **full cock**, at which point the gun was ready to fire. The act of pulling on the trigger would cause the hammer to spring forward. The hammer, which contained a piece of flint, would then strike another piece of flint locked beside the powder chamber. When the two flints struck each other it caused a spark; this in turn ignited the powder, which fired the ball. On occasions if the gun was set to half cock and it received a sudden shock or jolt it could prematurely release the hammer and so set off the gun.

The bitter end

Meaning something that is disappointing. On board ships one method of securing a rope is to wrap it around two wooden or metal posts attached to the deck. These posts are called **bitts**. The end part of the rope that was used to turn around the bitts is called the **bitter**. Despite the fact that it could be quite obvious to an observer that there was insufficient rope to make something secure some sailors would just keep on turning the rope up, perhaps in the vain hope it would do the job. When the rope ran out it was then said to have reached its **bitter end**.

Pulling someone's leg

The connection between this expression and its origin is not readily apparent, but nowadays it is used to mean **teasing someone**.

If a sailor, or other person for that matter, had the misfortune to be sentenced to death by hanging, the process could be a long-drawn-out affair. On ships the poor sailor would have a rope placed around his neck and would then be hoisted aloft. Death was usually due to strangulation rather than severing the spinal cord. In order to relieve the condemned man of his suffering, colleagues would often reach up and give his leg a sharp pull. This would hopefully put the poor chap out of his misery in a more expeditious manner.

The talkback

Prior to the re-engining of the *QE2* in 1989 the ship was equipped with a steam turbine propulsion unit. The engine room spaces were separated into three main sections, the main control room, the turbine control and the boiler room. Obviously it was essential to be able to communicate rapidly and clearly between each of these spaces.

> THOUGHT FOR THE DAY
> **Always remember you're unique.**
> **Just like everyone else**
> PO'S

On one occasion a problem developed with the talkback system between the main control room and the boiler room. An electrician was called and he began investigations into the cause of the fault.

After making a few adjustments the electrician pushed the call button connecting the boiler room, and asked the duty engineer to give him a test call. As no one ever knows what to say for a test call the world standard seems to be 'Testing $1 - 2 - 3 - 4 - 5 - 6$', and this is exactly how the engineer made his call. After a few more adjustments the electrician asked for a repeat call and in a rather bored voice the response was 'Testing $6 - 5 - 4 - 3 - 2 - 1$'.

Immediately the call was completed the electrician told the engineer that he must have got his wires crossed as the numbers were now coming out backwards.

'No no,' replied the engineer, 'that was me.'

Rubbing salt into old wounds

As mentioned previously, salt was a valuable commodity around the beginning of the first millennium – not least due to its preservative and antiseptic properties. Since many soldiers and sailors forming the Roman Legions were paid in salt (**salary**) it was considered too valuable a commodity to waste on trivial matters. After a battle, with many combatants injured, it rankled when relatively minor wounds were treated with salt. The amount used was frequently subjected to some creative accounting and naturally deducted from the hard-earned salary of the soldier (some things do not change). In other cases, salt was used to treat wounds that were already well on the way to healing (old wounds), which was felt by many to be even more of a waste of time and expense.

Poop deck

That area of a ship located towards the aft end.

The word **poop** is very simply derived from the Latin *puppis*, meaning stern. However, on further investigation, if we take the word *puppis* it has a strong similarity to the English word for a young dog or **puppy**. Nearly all ships carried a number of animals on board, either as pets or as a means of fresh food. As with all animals, they required an area to be set aside for their natural functions. Most ships preferred to use the after part of the vessel for this purpose. So, as the term most commonly used to describe the animal waste is of course **poop** (and the implement used for the removal of the waste is a *pooper-scooper*), we can only conjecture that this is how the word came into being.

There may well be other plausible explanations. I will leave it up to the reader to decide if this version is authentic.

The salute

It is generally agreed (by me anyway) that the salute developed from the days of King Arthur and his Knights of the Round Table.

It is also believed that most knights spent most of their time riding around the country slaying dragons and rescuing damsels in distress. Should two knights chance to meet, each would lift the visor of his helmet in order to expose his face to the other. If they then recognised each other, they would perhaps stop and have a chat before carrying on with their respective journeys. On the other hand, if they did not recognise each other, it is possible that a duel would take place – provided of course there was an audience.

In the army, a soldier raises his right arm to his forehead in a similar fashion of greeting, but also to show the other person he is unarmed and so does not present an immediate threat.

On the other hand, sailors were allowed to use either hand when saluting. This was based on the assumption that if the right hand was engaged in hauling on a rope or perhaps assisting the sailor in hanging on for dear life, it would have been decidedly inconvenient for him to let go.

Quarter master

In the modern merchant navy the term quarter master refers to a seaman who is skilled in the art of steering and looking after the area of the bridge.

On board His Britannic Majesty's sailing ships the quarter deck was an area of the ship reserved for the officer class. While most of these gentlemen possessed many of the necessary social graces, a number were less skilled at performing at least some of the more practical seamanship duties. Certain ordinary sailors, who were quite proficient at these tasks, were therefore allowed onto the quarter deck to 'assist' the officers. Over a period of time their expertise became recognised and they became known as Masters of the Quarter Deck.

Sound advice

Never go into a strange harbour on a falling tide without a pilot.

Marooned

A form of punishment handed out on board ships to any crew or person found to have misbehaved or just been downright unpopular. It is believed to have originated from the time a group of Cameroon natives were unceremoniously dumped on an island in the Caribbean and left to fend for themselves. It is claimed that Sir Francis Drake discovered them, gave them water and food, then returned them to their home-land, which act of charity earned him their eternal gratitude.

The word has also been used in a more modern context by some Scottish people wishing to purchase a round of drink.

Smoking

Smoking has always attracted controversy, particularly with the captain of a certain cargo ship en route to New Zealand.

Not only did he disapprove of smoking, he went so far as to ban smoking on the bridge. One afternoon, the officer standing the 12 – 4 watch felt the urge for a cigarette. Knowing that all good captains have a sleep in the afternoon, he gathered his sextant, went out onto the bridge wing while waiting for the sun to appear, and decided to risk a quick smoke. Hardly had he lit up when, out of the corner of his eye, he saw the captain entering the bridge. Without a moment's hesitation he immediately threw his very expensive sextant over the ship's side.

Note: A sextant is a very precise piece of navigational equipment used for measuring the angle of celestial bodies above the horizon. This angle, together with the exact time, can be used in calculating a ship's position.

Still more questions passengers have asked

Do these stairs go up?

I'm married but can I go to the singles party?

Does the sun always rise on the left-hand side of the ship?

Is the doctor qualified?

Will I get wet if I go snorkeling?

Why don't we have a late-night comedy spot in the afternoon?

Can I please have some hot iced tea?

Why aren't the dancers fully dressed?

How does the captain know which port to go to?

Does this elevator go up as well as down?

Are there two seatings at the midnight buffet?

Do we have to stay up until midnight to change our clocks?

Spick and span

Used to describe something that is all neat and tidy. **Spick** was the name given to the nails used to secure the timber planks on board ship, while **span** is another word for the actual timbers. The original expression is believed to have been **spick and span new**, meaning the ship was brand new, direct from the builder's yard. The word **new** was subsequently dropped and the revised term became synonymous with anything that looked new or well maintained.

Filibuster

From the French word **filibustier**, meaning to obtain plunder for personal gain by holding up and robbing the unwary. Originally adopted by the British and used to describe those seafarers who plundered and stole from shipping on the high seas (in other words pirates). Of course the British did not refer to themselves as pirates, preferring the more romantic and swashbuckling term **buccaneers**.

Today **filibuster** is used to describe parliamentarians who, for whatever reason, use stalling tactics to **hold up** or stall the introduction of various legislative bills – maybe in the hope of personal gain.

Baggage only

On board *Caronia* the majority of cabins are equipped with twin beds. Prior to embarkation, the bedroom staff would place a folded canvas cover on one of the beds in order to protect the bed linen from damage by suitcases. The cover was meant to be unfolded, spread over the bed and, once the unpacking process was completed, the room steward would then remove the cover and keep it safe and ready for the next time.

Not long after one particular embarkation, the duty receptionist on the front desk was approached by a very irate passenger who proceeded to complain loudly that he was a regular passenger on cruise ships and he had specifically booked a room with twin beds, for himself and his wife. He was now very upset to find that Cunard had assigned him a room with only one single bed. The receptionist looked up the room details and, as she suspected, it was listed as having twin beds. As reason did not seem to be working the receptionist contacted the Executive House-keeper and together they set off to examine the cabin.

One can only imagine how the passenger felt when it was explained that you could actually remove the canvas sheet and use the bed underneath for sleeping.

Ensigns

The Red Ensign was first flown by the Royal Navy in 1625 and, for some reason unknown to me, was used by the Merchant Navy shortly after that time. Around 1650 the Royal Navy felt the need to fly all three ensigns in use at the time, namely the Red, the Blue and the White. These different-coloured ensigns were used to distinguish between the different naval squadrons in operation. This practice remained in force until 1864.

After 1864 the Red Ensign was dedicated solely for use by the Merchant Navy, the White Ensign was assigned to the Royal Navy and the Blue Ensign was flown by ships attached to the Royal Naval Reserve. Just to complicate matters, Merchant Navy ships may fly the Blue Ensign if the captain and at least six other persons on board are members of the RNR. The White Ensign may be flown by the Royal Yacht Squadron. All yachts flying flags other than the Red Ensign must be in possession of a special Admiralty Warrant.

Confused? Now we can move onto defaced ensigns – another time.

Loggerheads

If a person is said to be ***at loggerheads*** with someone it generally indicates that the two people have had some sort of a disagreement or are on opposite sides in an argument.

When it became necessary on board a ship to repair the caulking or tar seams fitted between the deck planks they would use an implement called a ***loggerhead*** (I have no idea where that name came from). This tool consisted of two round metal balls, each attached at the opposite end of a wooden handle. Each ball was heated in rotation over an open fire until red hot. The hot end would be placed into a bucket of tar, causing the tar to melt. The melted tar was then much easier to apply to the deck seams.

Caulking was a messy job, not at all popular, as the tar would stick to skin, clothing and anything else it came in contact with, which could cause sailors to become short-tempered with each other. If tempers rose sufficiently it was not uncommon for one or both of the men to use the loggerhead as a form of weapon. Sometimes this form of combat was referred to as getting ***pitched into*** each other – pitch being another word for tar.

Dinghy

The name given to a small type of boat propelled either by sails or by oars. Like a number of words in common usage today this one originated from the time ships traded with the East Indies. When ships anchored off many of the ports of India, small local boats would be used to ferry the sailors to and from the shore. These boats were referred to by the Hindi word **dingi**. It is presumed that as this was an easy name to roll off the tongue the name stuck and came into use for smaller types of boats back in England.

Wardroom

The name of a room on board ship where the officers can dine, relax and socialise, mostly used on naval ships but occasionally on some of the grander passenger liners and cargo ships.

The name originates from a room where officers kept their spare clothing and uniforms, known as the wardrobe room – the word **ward** meaning to guard or keep, while robes referred to clothing. If officers wanted to meet somewhere where they could have a quiet chat it became the custom to go to the **wardrobe room**. Over the years the room changed from being a sort of clothing store to more of a recreational area; tables were fitted for dining and a bar was installed. Being a bit of a mouthful, especially after a glass or two of wine, the **wardrobe room** quickly became shortened to the **wardroom**.

Chewing the fat

An odd sort of expression often used to describe a couple of people chatting away, mainly about nothing.

Without the benefit of refrigeration, early ships relied on salted beef as part of their staple diet, and not generally the best cuts at that. This meant the meat was extremely tough and took quite a bit of chewing in order to get it to a state where it could be swallowed and digested.

To help pass the time while chewing the poor-quality and often fatty meat, the sailors would often engage in idle conversation, as the two jaw movements tended to complement each other.

A loose cannon

Someone who is out of control.

One of the most feared things that could happen on a warship, apart from getting into battle, was for a cannon to break loose from its lashings during a storm. The cannon were extremely heavy, and once they started to move were almost impossible to stop. It was not unknown for loose cannon to be the cause of the complete destruction of a ship as they smashed from side to side puncturing the wooden planking.

Pull your finger out

To hurry up or get a move on.

On board a man o' war, when preparing cannon for firing a small amount of gunpowder was poured into the vent hole at the rear of the barrel. This was in effect the ignition source for the main charge of gunpowder. In order to prevent this powder blowing away in the breeze a sailor would be delegated the task of placing his finger over the vent hole until such time as the gun was to be fired. When that time came the gun captain would 'request' the appointed sailor to pull his finger out, or in other words get on with the job at hand.

Clewed-up

Someone who is fully aware of what is going on. The reverse is someone who hasn't a clue, no idea what is going on and is liable to react unpredictably.

In order to control the tension and angle of a sail a small eyelet is sewn into the lower aft corner of the sail, a device known as a *clew*. Ropes or *sheets* are then attached to the clew and are used to make any required adjustments. If the clew is damaged or missing it becomes very difficult to control the sail and, therefore, the movement of the ship. A knowledgeable observer seeing a ship with sails flying and steering on an erratic course might easily remark that the ship had become *clewless*.

Voyage into the unknown

The Puritans loaded more beer than water onto the *Mayflower* before they departed for the New World.

Burial at sea

It was long a tradition that anyone having the misfortune to pass away on board ship was buried at sea, wrapped up in an old canvas sail. This duty was performed by the ship's sailmaker.

As medical knowledge was not always that proficient, there were occasions when people were buried at sea without actually being dead. In order to reduce the chance of this serious error occurring, the last stitch of the canvas was always placed through the nose of the deceased – considered a sensitive part of the body. Should the sailor suddenly sit up and scream he was then removed from the canvas and returned to his duties.

It was the custom to give the sailmaker a tot of rum on completion of this gruesome task.

Touch wood

A sign or gesture that is made when someone is hoping for the satisfactory outcome of an event.

Seamen are, by nature, a very superstitious group of individuals who also have an unshakable belief in the hereafter. One origin for this gesture was that as ships were made almost entirely of wood, touching the wooden structure of the ship confirmed that the timber was sound, free from defects and therefore strong enough to see you through any adversity. Another and perhaps more likely explanation comes from the time of the of the Crusades, when knights are thought to have carried a piece a wood on their persons when going into battle. This piece of wood was believed to be a part of the True Cross of Christ. It led to a lively trade in the sale of relics for this purpose.

Swinging the lead

This expression is probably better known on the eastern side of the Atlantic, again owing its origin to the heady days of sail.

If someone is said to be swinging the lead it generally refers to a person who is pretending to work or skiving away from work.

As ships spent long periods of time in uncharted waters, it was considered an advantage if they knew how deep the water was in front of them (in fact, it still is). In order to do this, they placed a man in the front of the ship and gave him a long line with a lead weight attached to the end. The line was marked with different colours and different types of material so the leadsman could tell how deep the line went into the water before touching bottom.

On long passages, a man could spend days throwing the line into the water and never touch bottom. It could be quite boring and tiresome having to haul the lead weight back on board many, many times, so, when the leadsman thought the ship was in deep water he would often not bother to throw the line. Rather he would just swing it back and forward as if doing his job, then every few minutes or so he would shout out 'No bottom found'. The penalty for getting caught swinging the lead was up to twenty lashes of the cat o' nine tails.

Square meal

A description of a good and wholesome meal.

In the seventeenth century, and even today in some cases, food at sea was not necessarily of the highest quality. Breakfast and the midday meal would usually consist of a slice or two of bread, perhaps some cheese if you were lucky and liquid refreshment to wash it all down.

In order to keep body and soul together, a much more substantial meal was served in the evening, which would include meat (of varying quality). As the quantities served in the evening were much larger, a tray was required to hold all the food. For ease of stowage, trays were of a square shape – and hence evolved the term a **square meal**.

The postcard

When visiting countries that are perhaps foreign to our guests it is always a concern for the ship's staff to make sure all of our guests make it safely back to the ship and in plenty of time before sailing. One enterprising cruise director devised an extremely useful guide for passengers and was in the habit of sharing this advice at the beginning of each cruise.

Before going ashore, he would advise each passenger, take a postcard showing a picture of the ship. If they then found themselves in a situation where they were lost and time was running out, they could hail a taxi. If the driver could not speak their language, they should show him the picture of the ship and get a lift back.

When the time came to sail from the port of Cadiz, we knew that there was still one passenger missing. As her husband was on board, we felt it worthwhile just waiting for a few extra minutes in the hope the lady would soon appear.

Sure enough, just as we were getting ready to let go the mooring lines, a taxi came hurtling down the dockside – coming to a screeching halt by the gangway – and a rather harassed-looking lady leapt out. Thankful that she had returned safely, we landed the gangway and sailed for our next port.

When asked what had happened, she explained that following the cruise director's advice, she had a postcard of the ship in her handbag. When the time approached for sailing she had hailed a taxi but, as the driver could not speak any English, she had shown him a photograph of the ship and indicated that she was in a hurry. The driver set off at full speed, drove all around the city and eventually pulled up outside the main post office several miles from the dock. The driver, looking very proud of himself, then indicated to the lady whether she wished him to wait while she posted the card.

Cloud nine

To be happy and at peace with the world.

In 1896 clouds were divided up into ten basic types according to their form, height and shape. Cloud number 9, **cumulonimbus**, was classified as 'tall' and estimated to tower above thirty to forty thousand feet. The cloud's shape is large and fluffy with a soft, comfortable appearance as it floats freely and gracefully across the sky. Hence, if someone was said to be **on cloud 9**, they were considered to be happy and at peace with the world – which belies the fact that inside the body of the cloud there can be violent winds with dense hailstorms.

THOUGHT FOR THE DAY

Before you criticise someone, you should walk a mile in their shoes. That way, when you criticise them, you're a mile away and you have their shoes.

PO'S

Cut of his jib

'I do not like the cut of his jib' means I do not like the look of something or someone.

During times of war one of the most effective methods of controlling the opposing navy was to hold a blockade. This effectively forced the opposition to remain within the confines of port, making them to all intents and purposes useless.

Maintaining a blockade was not necessarily an easy thing to accomplish, as the wind had a habit of blowing the ships in directions they did not necessarily want to go. In order to give a greater degree of control some captains would reduce the size of the jib sail by cutting it much smaller than would normally be used for regular sailing. Any ship approaching another ship that had her jib trimmed would immediately arouse suspicion.

Seasickness

Ginger has been clinically demonstrated to work twice as well as Dramamine for fighting motion sickness.

A glass or two of port and brandy has been known to settle a churning stomach. Whether this actually alleviates the symptoms or just helps take your mind off the malaise is not clear.

Wristbands work for some people, while behind-the-ear patches work for others.

My favourite cure, attributed to Sir Isaac Newton, is to **sit under a tree**. (I understand oak trees are the most effective.)

Under the weather

We use this term to describe someone who is unwell.

On board ship, one of the least favourite lookout positions was on the bow on the windward or weather side. During periods of inclement weather, this position was pretty miserable, with the lookout getting continually soaked by the cold, harsh spray, often causing him to become unwell.

Run the gauntlet

In today's terms to **run the gauntlet** means to take a chance or a calculated risk, failure having the potential to be particularly unpleasant.

On board His Majesty's ships in the seventeenth and eighteenth centuries, theft was considered a particularly heinous crime. It still is on board ships where we live and work in such close proximity with our colleagues.

Should a sailor be accused of stealing, one form of punishment was **running the gauntlet**. This was where two rows of men lined up, each man armed with a special rope end. The victim was made to walk between the lines of sailors. In order to prevent the accused from speeding down the line too quickly, a Master at Arms would slowly walk in front with his sword strategically placed at the offender's breast. The accused was then subject to a beating from his shipmates.

The clever thing about this form of punishment is that, ships being small, compact communities, it was very likely that his colleagues would have a pretty good idea if the person was guilty of the offence, which might not always have been apparent to his superiors. If his colleagues thought he was innocent. then the beating would be quite lenient. On the other hand, if they believed him to be guilty ...

Divert your course

The following is an actual radio conversation released by the US Chief of Naval Operations on 10 October 1995. I have heard similar versions attributed to various navies.

Navy: Please divert your course 15 degrees to the north to avoid a collision.

Civilian: Recommend you divert YOUR course 15 degrees to south to avoid a collision.

Navy: This is the Captain of a US Navy ship. I say again, divert YOUR course.

Civilian: No. I say again, you divert YOUR course.

Navy: This is the aircraft carrier *Enterprise*. We are a large warship of the US Navy. Divert your course now!

Civilian: This is a lighthouse. Your call.

Rummage sale

Name given to a sale of goods not considered to be of any real value.

The word **rummage** is derived from the old French word **arrumage**, meaning the stowage of ships' cargo. Cargo which had been damaged and subsequently rejected by the intended owner was often placed on sale so that the shipper or insurance agent could at least recoup some of his losses.

Scraping the bottom of the barrel

A last resort.

Slush is the residue left in a barrel of salted meat once the contents have been removed. Since the slush was a particularly obnoxious substance, it was generally felt that someone had to be pretty desperate to go to all the trouble to collect the contents. Impoverished ships' cooks were often seen to collect the slush, and while in theory this was

the property of the captain, they would often sell the residue on to candle makers for a small sum of money, which was then used to supplement their meagre income.

It is unlikely that the skilled and highly paid chefs on today's passenger ships would pursue such a custom, even if it were still an option. On the other hand, poorly paid captains might ...

The powder room

The Island of St Kitts in the northern part of the Caribbean is famous, among other things, for the old fort on Brimstone Hill. Cruise ships regularly run tours to the fort and allow guests to spend time roaming around the grounds to examine the various structures, buildings and artefacts. The fort, built in the sixteenth century, has a colourful history, having been under the control of the English, then the French, then back to the English, and probably at some time under Spanish rule, down through the centuries.

As the ship sailed that evening the captain joined his table in the restaurant for the usual evening meal and, as most people do, enquired how his table companions had enjoyed their day on the island.

One American lady was quite enthused by her visit to the old fort and spent some time describing her experience to her table guests, ending with how she thought it was so wonderful that all those years ago, the fort builders and soldiers went to so much trouble to look after the welfare and personal hygiene of those in the fort, especially the ladies.

Not quite comprehending where the lady was coming from, the captain asked her to explain what she meant. The lady went on to say that, as they walked around the inside of the fort, they had come across a large room with faded sign carved above the door: POWDER ROOM.

It fell to one of the other table guests to explain that the room may possibly have been used for the storage of gunpowder rather than somewhere for the Ladies to prepare themselves for Dinner.

A bit of a flap

Generally meaning some sort of panic.

Flags on board ships are colloquially said to *flap* and for centuries were used as the main form of communication between ships at sea.

As late as the First World War, when the British fleet was at anchor in Scapa Flow, Admiral Jellico gave the order to intercept and attack the German fleet at Jutland, by hoisting signal flags visible to the entire fleet. A couple of ratings looked at the flags and were heard to remark: 'Looks like there is a bit of a flap on.'

Round robin

A type of letter or other communication that is signed by a number of people.

In the Navy, when the crew were unhappy about conditions on board their ship, they often communicated their feelings by writing a letter to the captain. This could have serious repercussions for whoever initiated the letter or was the first signature on the form. In order to apportion the blame equally, or better still not at all, each crew member would sign his name so that all the names formed a circle. Where the word *robin* came from nobody is quite sure but it alliterates nicely with *round*.

Log book

On board early sailing ships, the most common method of recording information was to take a suitable piece of wood or log and trim off a section in the form of a tablet or shingle. These tablets were then bound together and made into a book. Important information concerning the progress of the voyage was then transcribed onto the shingle, making it into a permanent record.

With the invention of paper, a gradual transformation was made towards this new form of writing material. It did, however, take a number of centuries for paper to replace the time-honoured shingles as they did not react well with the wet and windy conditions all too frequently encountered at sea.

Navy blue

In 1745, a group of officers met and decided that the time had come to have a standard design and colour for the uniform worn by His Majesty's Officers at Sea.

The First Lord of the Admirality, being somewhat indecisive, gathered together those officers involved, and had them model the various proposals. He then selected a few possibilities and had these shown to King George II for his decision. The King was also unable to make up his mind and so, after much deliberation, he chose the blue and white combination as these were the favourite colours of the wife of the First Lord of the Admiralty, the Duchess of Bedford.

One can only speculate ...

What's in a name?

As an additional service and a way of earning a little extra revenue, organised tours are offered to the guests at each port the ship visits. On board *Caronia*, it was always our custom to provide members of the ship's staff as escorts, just in case something should go wrong.

When visiting Vigo on the northwestern coast of Spain, guides were in short supply and so we asked lecturers, hosts and anyone else who was not officially classed as a passenger to help out.

One gentleman volunteered to escort a city tour, and his offer was quickly accepted. The group was duly sent on its four-hour sightseeing trip. About mid-way through the tour there was the usual 'comfort break' and the chance to do some shopping. For some reason, the tour escort managed to get separated from the main group and found himself alone with no idea where he was, or how to get back to the ship. Hailing a passing taxi, he gave the driver the name of the ship: 'the *Caronia*'. The driver seemingly understood and set off on the trip. After about forty minutes, the passenger started to become a little concerned, as they appeared to be in open country. After a further ten minutes he became really concerned and asked the driver to stop. He repeated, 'The *Caronia*, the *Caronia*.' '*Si, si*,' said the driver, producing a map and pointing to **La Coruña** – a Spanish city some eighty miles to the north of Vigo.

Sadly, as a result of the error, he missed the ship and had to spend a considerable sum of money to fly to our next port of call at Malaga.

Limeys

An American slang term for British sailors.

Scurvy was the scourge of the navy. After prolonged periods at sea, a sailor's health could seriously deteriorate to the point were teeth would fall out, gums would bleed and the skin would develop all kinds of unpleasant sores. It took a number of centuries before the cause was fully understood and found to be an acute lack of vitamin C.

In the West Indies, where many ships traded, limes were plentiful, and these contained ample quantities of natural vitamin C. If the limes were crushed and mixed with sugar, which was also in plentiful supply, a long-lasting, sweet and healthy drink was produced. In 1795 lime juice was made part of the normal supply of rations on all British ships and virtually eradicated the disease overnight.

Other navies throughout the world apparently knew of the

advantages of eating their fruit and greens long before the British, and that is why the Americans appeared to be so amused by this particular British trait.

Letting the cat out of the bag

Back in the days of sailing ships, discipline was often harsh and severe. Sometimes it also became necessary to encourage some poor matelot to divulge information he might otherwise be reluctant to do.

The most common form of punishment in the seventeenth and eighteenth centuries was the cat of nine tails. This was basically a length of rope which had nine 18-inch lengths of lighter rope woven into the main body, or handle. Each of the nine strands had three knots.

The poor soul was tied up to gratings, arms outstretched with his back laid bare. Punishment commenced on the utterance of the immortal words, 'Let the cat out of the bag.'

As a way of making the punishment even more effective, the poor recipient often had to fabricate the very object of his demise, complete with a hand-crafted canvas bag. All of which had to be submitted for quality control prior to use.

The **cat o' nine tails** is connected to the myth that a cat has **nine lives**, but I am not exactly sure how.

The practice of using the cat was outlawed by the British Navy in 1879.

Pass with flying colours

Ships at sea identify themselves by flying the flag or colours of the nation to which they belong. In times of conflict, any ship belonging to a nation with whom you were at war was considered fair game and could be attacked. The rewards for capturing an enemy ship could be quite significant.

As a means of self-preservation, if a particular ship did not wish to engage the enemy, they would often fly the same flag as the approaching vessel in the hope they would be allowed to pass unmolested.

On the other hand, some ships would fly the colours of the approaching enemy to lull them into a false sense of security and so try to give themselves the advantage during an attack.

It is difficult to believe that the British Navy would resort to such underhand practices ...

THOUGHT FOR THE DAY
If you lend someone £20 and never see that person again, it was probably worth it

PO'S

Weather eye

To keep a weather eye open means to keep a sharp look out for any approaching trouble.

Wind direction can be simplified into two main directions: **up wind** (or the **weather side**) and **down wind** (or the **leeward side**). Up wind is the direction the weather is coming from, and down wind the direction it is going to.

As most sailors have two eyes, the simple way of making sure someone was looking out for any adverse weather conditions was to have him keep one eye open on the weather side of the ship.

Keel-hauling

A very severe form of punishment at sea originated by the Dutch during the fifteenth and sixteenth centuries. Other countries, including Britain, also adopted this form of punishment.

A seaman found guilty of some serious crime at sea would be strung up by his arms from the main yard, with another rope tied to his feet and passed under the keel of the boat, up the other side and attached to the opposite yard. On a given signal a chosen group of sailors would release the poor seaman so that he dropped into the water. They would then haul him to the other side of the ship, dragging him under the keel.

If the ship had been at sea for a long period of time the bottom was most likely covered with razor-sharp barnacles. If the sailor did not drown during this punishment, it was more than likely that the journey across the barnacles would be his undoing.

Dead wood

Something that serves no useful purpose. Claimed to originate from the practice of placing sturdy blocks of timber between the frames on the keel of a ship. These blocks served no other useful purpose than to strengthen that part of the ship.

Personally, I would have considered that quite a useful attribute.

Tickety boo

A light-hearted slang expression to mean everything is just fine. It would appear to emanate from the maritime trade between India and the United Kingdom. As sailors plied their trade in far-off lands, they would use local labour for the numerous tasks involved in general shipboard operations. These jobs were much sought-after and, in order to retain this valuable position, many would respond to questions in a more positive manner than perhaps might have been the case. The local expression in Hindi, **tikai babu**, meaning 'it is all right, sir', was much favoured and was quickly adopted by the western sailor to mean everything was proceeding as planned.

Up through the hawse pipe

In the forward part of the ship there is a large tube or pipe used for running out the anchor cable or hawser. This pipe extends from the forward deck of the ship to the outside part just above the waterline.

If a sailor was said to have come up through the hawse pipe it would mean that he was someone who started life at sea at the bottom of the working ladder and gradually worked his way up. Many a captain, even today, is said to have come up through the hawse pipe.

Mess room

The name given to the room where officers and crew take their meals.

On first hearing the word you could be forgiven for assuming that it referred to the state of cleanliness in which these areas were sometimes found. Once again, however, we owe the origin of this word to the French, who apparently borrowed it from the Latin. It has since been adopted into other languages, including German and Spanish. Various spellings of the word including *mes*, *messus* and *meschen* all refer to food or the act of eating food in a group.

Long shot

A term used mainly by gamblers when the odds of something turning out in their favour are not all that good and luck is expected or hoped to play a part.

During the seventeenth and eighteenth centuries, cannon were far from accurate, especially at any sort of distance and particularly on a moving ship. If the decision was taken to try taking a shot at a distant enemy it was considered more good luck than skill if a hit was scored.

There is of course another side to this. The more you practise, the luckier you become.

German mile

Not by a German mile is a strange sort of expression not much used today but quite common a couple of hundred years ago. It was used to describe something that was a long way off the mark or far away.

In the seventeenth century, German mathematicians introduced a new means of calculating distances at sea, based on the nautical mile but four times longer. There is a degree of logic to this when you take into account celestial time and the spherical shape of the earth. Dutch navigators adopted this system for a few decades but it never really caught on and quickly fell into disuse.

My own theory about its origin is that since a German mile is longer that the nautical mile there were fewer of them between points on the surface of the earth, and therefore it did not take so long to travel around the world. Logical really.

Red herring

Meaning something that is designed to deceive.

With their well-known powers of smell, dogs were often used as a means of tracking down criminals and poachers. In order to put the dogs off the scent, rather old and smelly herring were placed along various escape routes. The dogs tended to follow the strongest scent, which allowed the crafty offender to evade capture.

Opportunity

It is perhaps not surprising that we are in debt to the Romans for the origin of a number of words in everyday use in our language. Combine that with the traditions of seafaring, and history can start to take on a completely different meaning.

In the early days of sail, a ship's arrival time at port was often governed by the state of the tide. It still is in many cases. If the tide was too low then the ship would have to wait outside the port until conditions improved. The word **ob** translated from ancient Roman means more or less 'to stand off waiting'. Combine this with **port** and we get standing off port, waiting for the right moment. Hence **opportunity** has come to mean waiting for the right moment.

By guess and by God

Seafarers have throughout the ages been a deeply religious group of adventurers, motivated no doubt by the high mortality rate found at sea. Navigation was for centuries a black art, inspired by experience, a degree of mathematical skill and an unswerving faith in the Supreme Being. In other words the art of determining one's position at sea was frequently achieved more **by guess and by God** than by any other reliable method.

Junk

Equipment that no longer serves any useful purpose.

On board ships, when rope, cordage and old sails had served their purpose they were referred to as *junk*. As these items fell under the collective responsibility of the mate he would often sell these bits and pieces on to a junkman, of which there was always one to be found in every port.

By hook or by crook

By one way or another.

Attributed to Oliver Cromwell, who in 1649 planned a campaign to sack the city of Waterford situated on the southern coast of Ireland.

Waterford can be approached from the sea by entering between two headlands, **Crook** on the Waterford side and **Hook** on the Wexford side. Apparently when asked how he proposed to take the city his reply was vague: 'By Hook or by Crook.' Either he didn't want to give too much away or at the time he hadn't quite made up his mind.

A couple of shakes

A short period of time.

Steering a ship close to the wind required a certain degree of concentration. The longer a helmsman had been steering, the more likely he was to lose his concentration. If that happened and the ship turned, putting her head into the wind, the forward sails would flap or shake.

Towards the end of a long watch the relief knew it was time to report for duty if he heard a couple of shakes of the sail. It was not unknown for a helmsman to deliberately cause the sails to shake in order to try and get an early relief or just to remind the next man it was his time.

Toasts at sea

In Nelson's day the rituals surrounding the consumption of alcohol played an important role in the life of the seaman, whether to relieve the boredom or simply to disguise the miserable conditions is not quite clear.

It has long been the custom when collectively enjoying a social cocktail to drink a toast to something or someone, probably as some form of attempt to justify the occasion. The Navy has been credited with leading the way in this custom, having listed a different toast for each day of the week. The following are generally agreed as the daily toasts originating in Nelson's day and still practised on some ships to this day (but not, I hasten to add, with the same quantities of alcohol):

Monday night –   Our ships at sea

Tuesday night –   Our men

Wednesday night –   Ourselves

Thursday night –   A bloody war or a sickly season

Friday night –   A willing foe and sea room

Saturday night –   Sweethearts and wives

Sunday night –   Absent friends

It is another naval tradition that **toasts** may be taken and given while remaining in the seated position. This is alleged to stem from an occasion in 1660 when King Charles II was on board His Majesty's Ship *Naseby*. While attempting to stand in preparation for making a toast the good King bumped his head on the low ceiling. Being King, he immediately issued a Royal Proclamation that forthwith all toasts on board His Majesty's ships should be taken while seated – a tradition that remains until the present day. The only exception is that all must stand during the playing of the National Anthem. Presumably this was because the King himself would not have to stand and so would not run the risk of repeating his injury.

SOS

The universal signal sent out by ships when they were in distress. Many think that the letters SOS stand for the phrase ***Save Our Souls*** but this is not at all the case. After the invention of Morse code by Samuel Morse (some time between 1791 and 1872) the letters **SOS** were chosen quite simply because they had an easily identifiable sound that was simple for all to understand when converted into the code:

• • •   —   —   —   • • •

Get the sack

To be dismissed from employment.

It was not always easy to find men of quality to crew His Majesty's ships, especially during times of conflict. This could mean that, on occasions, some of the men employed fell somewhat below even the minimum standards required by some captains. Still, ships had to sail and a poor pair of hands was better than no hands at all.

At the end of a voyage, when it was possible to reduce the number of crew, the first to go would be those who failed to meet the minimum requirements. Rather than pay them off with any form of bounty, the practice was to have the bosun or other senior petty officer approach the sailor, hand him an old linen sack and just tell him to pack up his gear and leave. The modern-day equivalent is clearing your office desk on a Friday night.

This form of dismissal was nearly always done when the ship arrived in port. To do it earlier would be to court revenge should the seaman take exception to his dismissal – again much the same as the logic behind Friday-afternoon dismissals.

Sling your hook

Another and less formal method of conveying to a sailor that he was no longer required on board ship.

In order to rig a hammock there was a clew or ring fitted at each end. A rope was then secured to the clew while at the other end there was a hook for attaching to the ship. If someone was told to sling his hook it was just another way of telling him he was no longer required and that he should pack up his hammock and sleep elsewhere.

Today it is used by some people, especially those with a nautical background, to convey to others that they are unwelcome in the present company and should move on.

Hawser

A very thick rope used for anchoring, towing, or other heavy duty work. The word is a derivative of the old English word **halse**, meaning neck. A hawser was usually about the thickness of a man's neck.

Clean bill of health

Meaning whoever or whatever is being referred to is healthy and/or free of any defects.

During the seventeenth and eighteenth centuries many countries were concerned about the spread of diseases, and one of the most common methods of acquiring infections was from visiting ships. In order to reduce the likelihood of this happening, countries would insist that, before any ship arrived in port, it had to obtain a certificate from the previous port stating that that country was healthy and disease-free. This document was referred to as the **Bill of Health**.

In order to indicate that the ship was healthy before arriving in port they were required to fly a yellow code flag. This custom is still in existence today.

THOUGHT FOR THE DAY
A closed mouth gathers no foot
PO'S

Canvas

That time-tested material used to make the sails that have powered ships for centuries is made from the hemp plant. The name canvas is derived from the Greek word for hemp, **kannabis**, a plant well known to have properties other than for the manufacture of sails.

The daily service

Every cruise ship produces a daily programme listing all the 'what's to do' events on board, as well as other useful information. On days when the ship is due to arrive in port, somewhere towards the top of the sheet it usually names the port and the country the ship is visiting, together with the expected arrival time.

On one cruise from New York to New England the ship called at

Boston, Massachusetts before heading north to Newfoundland and beyond. During cruises, many people of the Roman Catholic faith appreciate having a daily mass and under normal circumstances these services are well attended.

On the morning in question, after the ship arrived in Boston, the poor front-desk receptionist was subjected to a very vociferous complaint from an irate passenger. It would seem that at 8 o'clock this particular passenger had gone to the room normally set aside for church services, only to find that despite being advertised in the daily programme there was no service taking place. The receptionist, slightly confused, knew that we never held a service on days when the ship was in port as most of our guests preferred to go ashore but, just to make sure, she took a copy of the programme and carefully read through the daily list of events. Nowhere could she see a church service mentioned.

The passenger, still very upset, then produced his copy of the programme and, pointing to the top of the page, invited her to take a look. Sure enough, there it was:

0800: ship arrives in Boston – Mass.

Plain sailing

Something that is relatively simple or straightforward.

The mathematical calculations involved in determining how to get from one place to another on the surface of the earth can be extremely complex, not least due to the fact that the earth is round. Among his attributes a skilled navigator of the past would have had to master the art of spherical trigonometry. Something beyond the wit of many a navigator today.

Before the advent of accurate time-pieces and navigation tables, navigators found it much simpler to steer courses either east or west until reaching their intended longitude, then turning north or south in order to reach their final destination. While taking a bit longer it did eliminate the need to perform the more complicated calculations required when crossing the oceans at an angle.

Ode to a seaman

Between the innocence of infancy and the recklessness of adultery comes that unique specimen of humanity known as a seaman. Seamen can be found in bed, in arguments, in debt and intoxicated. They are tall, short, fat, thin, dark, fair but never normal.

They dislike ship's food, chief engineers, writing letters, sailing on Saturdays and dry ships. They like receiving mail, paying-off day, nude pin-ups, sympathy, complaining – and beer.

A seaman's secret ambition is to change places with the owner for just one trip, to own a brewery and to be loved by everyone in the world.

A seaman is a provider in war and a parasite in peace. No one is subjected to so much abuse, wrongly accused, so often misunderstood by so many, as a seaman.

He has the patience of Job, the honesty of a fool and the Heaven-sent ability to laugh at himself.

When a seaman returns home from a long voyage, no one else but a seaman can create such an atmosphere of suspense and longing as he walks in the door and is greeted with the immortal words ... *When do you go back?*

Diets

One should never underestimate the sailor's powers of observation. Over a number of centuries mariners have come to the following dietary conclusion:

The Japanese eat very little fat and suffer fewer heart attacks than the British.

The French eat a lot of fat and also suffer fewer heart attacks than the British.

The Italians drink excessive amounts of red wine but also suffer fewer heart attacks than the British.

The Germans, on the other hand, drink a lot of beer and eat lots of sausages and fats, but they also suffer fewer heart attacks than the British.

CONCLUSION: Eat and drink what you like. Speaking English is the problem.

Port hole

In modern terminology a port hole is an opening in the ship's side, fitted with a glass window. This kept the space inside waterproof yet let in the natural light. When King Henry VII was building his navy, he insisted that his ships had bigger and better cannon than his rivals, so much so that they became too big and too heavy to remain on the upper decks. In order to overcome this dilemma, his ship builders adopted an idea from a French ship builder (with the remarkably English name of James Baker). His idea was to place the cannon below deck but allow them to fire by constructing a waterproof opening or door in the ship's side. The French word for door is **porte** and so these, and any subsequent openings in the ship's side, became known as **port holes**.

Court martial

Should an Officer in His or Her Britannic Majesty's Navy be accused of an offence he would be entitled to trial by a panel of his peers, in other words a court martial.

On hearing all the evidence the distinguished panel would retire to consider their verdict. On reaching their conclusion the officer would then be summoned back to the courtroom to face the verdict. Prior to entering the room, it was the custom to place a sword on the table in front of the panel. If the hilt of the sword was facing the accused then he was innocent. Should the pointed end be facing the officer than his career could be assumed to have suddenly and dramatically taken a turn for the worse.

This custom is believed to have originated from the days when beheading was a common form of punishment. If a person were found guilty of a crime, the executioner's axe would be placed on a table with the cutting edge facing the accused. This would have left little doubt as to the fate of the guilty person.

Three sheets to the wind

This is an old nautical expression normally used to describe someone who is under the influence of alcohol and incapable of full control of his or her faculties. The expression in fact comes from sailing ships whose sails would normally have one or at most two sheets or ropes to control the sail. This expression is used when even if the person had the luxury of **three sheets**, he would still be unable to control the sail due to his intoxication.

Bermuda

Bermuda is one of the oldest colonies belonging to Britain and was first settled in 1609 after the British ship *Sea Venture*, commanded by Sir George Summers, was wrecked off the coast while on her way to Virginia. It is believed by many that it was this event that led Shakespeare to write *The Tempest* in 1611.

> THOUGHT FOR THE DAY
> **Generally speaking, you aren't learning much when your lips are moving**
> PO'S

Statues

If you see a statue of a person on a horse and the horse has both front legs in the air, it means that person died in battle.

If the horse has one front leg in the air the person died as a result of wounds received in battle.

If the horse has all four legs on the ground, the person died of natural causes.

One must assume that if all four legs are in the air it would indicate the horse is dead.

Qualifications required of a cruise ship officer

Based on a letter written by John Paul Jones in September 1775

It is by no means enough that an officer should be a capable mariner. He must be that, of course, but also a great deal more. He should be a gentleman of liberal education, refined manners, punctilious courtesy, and the nicest sense of personal honour. He should be the soul of tact, patience, justice, firmness, and charity. No meritorious act of a subordinate should escape his attention or be left to pass without its reward. Conversely, he should not be blind to a single fault in any subordinate, though, at the same time, he should be quick and unfailing to distinguish error from malice, thoughtlessness from incompetence, and well-meant shortcomings from stupidity.

The first sentence alone is a tough one.

And finally

Why I want to be a captain

Written by a 10-year-old American schoolboy and published in the newsletter of the Society of Marine Port Engineers of New York NY Inc.

I want to be a captain when I grow up because it's a funny job and easy to do. Captains don't need much school education, they just have to learn numbers so they can read the instruments. I guess they should be able to read maps so they don't get lost.

Captains have to be brave so they won't be scared if it's foggy and they can't see, or if a propeller falls off they should stay calm so they will know what to do. Captains have to have eyes to see through the clouds and they can't be afraid of thunder and lightning because they are closer to them than we are. The salary that captains make is another thing I like. They make more than they can spend. This is because most people think that captaining a ship is dangerous – except captains, because they know how easy it is.

There isn't much I don't like, except girls like captains and all the girls want to marry captains, so they always have to chase them away so they won't bother them. I hope I don't get seasick, because I get carsick and if I get seasick I could not be a captain and then I would have to go out to work.

Pretty well sums it up

CAPTAIN NICK BATES

Captain Nick is descended from two seafaring families. His father spent most of his adult life at sea and his grandfather on his mother's side was a traditional sailing-ship master.

He was born in Northern Ireland and brought up in the small fishing village of Ardglass. Educated in the farming town of Downpatrick, his academic achievements could at best be described as average. He did, however, go on to attend the Nautical College in Belfast, where he graduated top of his year. From there he joined Port Line, the cargo-ship subsidiary of Cunard Line, and began learning his trade on the UK to Australia, New Zealand run.

He obtained his 'Master's ticket' in 1975 and shortly afterwards was offered a position on board the luxury cruise liner *Queen Elizabeth 2*. Since that fateful day he has remained with the Passenger Division of Cunard Line.

Among his many hobbies and close to the top of the list is collecting useless information.

INDEX

UP THE CREEK
A lifetime spent trying
to be a sailor
Tony James

Up The Creek charts Tony James' unintentional voyage from his father's broad-bean bed, in land-locked Derbyshire, to a marina in Somerset via the Caribbean, the Persian Gulf and the bottom of a swimming pool in Ottery St Mary.

On the way Tony gathers a motley crew of unforgettable eccentrics and maritime misfits, brought to hilarious life by his acute observation of the ridiculous and by his wry acceptance that whatever happens at sea, things can only get worse. The funniest and most original sailing book for years.

Illustrated with photographs and drawings

'Laugh-out-loud funny ... unlike any other sailing memoir ... destined to become a classic'
Stephen Swann, Editor, *Traditional Boats and Tall Ships*

'Waves of humour in a sea of sailing experiences ... will delight sailors and landlubbers alike. Hugely entertaining'
Don Sutherland, Royal Yachting Association, International Sailing Federation Judge

'A comic masterpiece'
Martin Hesp, *Western Morning News*

UK   ISBN 0-9547062-7-7   £9.95 + p&p
USA ISBN 1-57409-222-7 $14.95 + p&p

THE WAPPING GROUP OF ARTISTS:
Sixty years of painting by the Thames

For sixty years, members of the Wapping Group have met to paint by the River Thames *en plein air*. Outdoors and undaunted in all weathers, come rain or shine, they have set up their easels from the broad tideways of the estuary to the willow-fringed

backwaters up-river – taking in the whole of riverside London in between.

With 200 illustrations, the story of the group since 1946, a meditation on the pleasures and pains of painting outdoors, and personal accounts by all the current members, this book captures the essence of the Wapping Group, "the last proper artists' society left in England".

'… a delight to the senses and an essential new addition for any bookshelf.'
E14 Magazine

'Sixty years after it was created, the Wapping Group is still flourishing and has won itself a secure niche in the artistic life of the capital …'
Classic Boat

UK   ISBN 0-9547062-5-0   £19.95 + p&p
USA ISBN 1-57409-218-9 $29.95 + p&p

ROUGH PASSAGE
Commander R. D. Graham

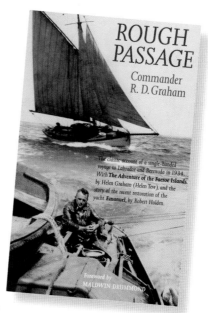

In 1934 Commander R. D. Graham sailed alone in his 30-foot yacht *Emanuel* from England to Newfoundland, cruised on the coast of Labrador, fell ill, sailed to Bermuda in November ('twenty-three days of uninterrupted misery'), wintered there, and finally brought his little vessel back across the Atlantic to her old moorings in Poole Harbour.

Also included is *The Adventure of the Faeroe Islands*, an account of *Emanuel*'s 1929 voyage by R. D. Graham's daughter Helen (later Helen Tew). But when it came to the transatlantic crossing, Commander Graham left his mate of many years behind. 'It seemed a particularly treacherous proceeding sailing off without her,' he wrote, and his daughter never forgave him until she too had crossed the Atlantic at the age of 88 – as described in her own book, *Transatlantic At Last*.

This new edition of the seafaring classic is brought up to date by Robert Holden's account of the recent restoration of *Emanuel*, allowing R. D. Graham's 'little yacht' to take her rightful place as part of Britain's maritime heritage.

This is a must-read for anyone with the slightest interest in the sea, or in human nature.

Illustrated with photographs

'One of the most remarkable small-boat adventures of this or any other time
Arthur Ransome

One of the 'great cruising accounts' listed in Peter Spectre's *A Mariner's Miscellany*

UK   ISBN 0-9547062-4-2   £9.95 + p&p
USA ISBN 1-57409-212-X $14.95 + p&p

THE LAST VOYAGE OF THE *LUCETTE*

Douglas Robertson

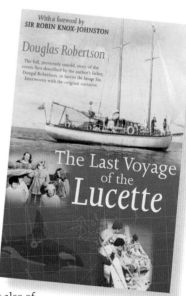

**With a foreword by
SIR ROBIN KNOX-JOHNSTON**

On board their 43-foot schooner *Lucette*,
the Robertson family set sail from the
south of England in January 1971. Eighteen
months out, in the middle of the Pacific,
Lucette was holed by killer whales and sank.
Four adults and two children survived the
next 38 days adrift, first in a survival raft,
then crammed into a 9-foot dinghy, before
being rescued by a Japanese fishing vessel.

This is the story of how they survived, but also of
the *Lucette*'s voyage across the Atlantic, around the Caribbean, through the Panama
Canal and out into the Pacific. It is a vivid and candid account of the delights and
hardships, the excitements and dangers, and the emotional highs and lows experienced by the family both before and after the shipwreck.

Douglas Robertson has taken his father's classic book *Survive the Savage Sea* as
his starting point, and has drawn upon a wealth of other sources, not least his own
memories of a life-changing experience, to bring us this true story of adventure, of
relationships strained to bursting point, of conflict and resolution.

Illustrated with photographs and drawings

'... awesome. A fantastic read and thoroughly
recommended.'
  Nautical Magazine

'A candid and highly coloured account of survival
in the teeth (quite literally) of the odds.'
  Lloyds List

| UK | ISBN 0-95427-508-x | £13.95 + p&p |
| USA | ISBN 1-57409-206-5 | $23.95 + p&p |